Maui

DIRECTIONS

WRITTEN AND RESEARCHED BY

Greg Ward

ROUGH
GUIDES

NEW YORK • LONDON • DELHI
www.roughguides.com

Contents

Introduction to

Maui

Thanks to its superb beaches, ravishing tropical scenery, exhilarating range of activities, and magnificent hotels, the island of Maui can justly claim to be the world's most glamorous vacation destination. The slogan Maui No Ka 'Oi – "Maui is the Best" – may gloss over the fact that it's both the second largest and the second youngest of the Hawaiian chain, and ranks a distant second to Oahu in terms of annual visitors, but for island inhabitants and devotees alike the "Valley Isle" has a cachet its neighbors could never match.

▼ Snorkeling off Maui

Maui is what's known as a "volcanic doublet," consisting of two originally separate but now overlapping volcanoes. The older of the two, known to geologists as Mauna Kahalawai, has eroded to

When to visit

Although Maui's high season for tourism is mid-December to March, its climate remains pretty constant year-round. Sea-level thermometers rarely drop below the low seventies Fahrenheit (around 22°C) in the daytime, or climb beyond the low eighties (around 28°C); at night the temperature seldom falls below the low sixties. Warm clothing is only necessary if you plan to drive up to the summit of Haleakalā; at dawn, the most popular time to visit, temperatures regularly drop below freezing.

In principle the rainiest months are from December to February, but where you are on the island makes far more difference than what time of year it is, and the main leeward tourist areas seldom receive more than the occasional light shower even then. The highest peak in the West Maui Mountains is deluged by over 400 inches of rain per year, but all the coastal resorts, including Kā'anapali, barely five miles away, get less than twenty inches.

Along protected stretches of the shoreline, you can expect to swim all year round in beautiful seas where the water temperature varies from 75°F to 82°F (24–28°C). Between October and April, however, high surf can render unsheltered beaches dangerous in the extreme.

▲ Green sea turtle

become a serrated ridge that's usually referred to as the West Maui Mountains; it's now dwarfed by the younger Haleakalā to the southeast. Haleakalā is not technically extinct, but only dormant, and may erupt again at some point in the future. Around four hundred thousand years ago, it dominated the landmass known as "Maui Nui," which incorporated what are now Kahoolawe, Molokai, and Lanai. Although the ocean has flowed in to create four distinct islands, the channels between them are the shallowest, and the calmest, in the state of Hawaii.

Because the tradewinds on Maui, like the rest of the state, blow consistently from the northeast, the island is much wetter on its north and east – windward – coasts, which are characterized by steep sea cliffs, inaccessible stream-cut valleys, and dense tropical vegetation, and has a drier and less fertile aspect on the west and south – leeward – sides. Indeed, each of its two distinct volcanoes has its own wet and dry sides.

Like its neighbors, Maui has concentrated almost all of its tourist development on its sunbaked leeward shorelines,

▼ Molokini

▲ Fruit stand on the road to Hāna

with its major resorts either lying north of historic Lahaina in West Maui, like Kāʻanapali and Kapalua, or along the southwestern flanks of Haleakalā in what's known as South Maui, like Kīhei, Wailua and Mākena.

These resorts offer safe beaches, ideal conditions for water sports, and all the amenities the modern vacationer could ask for. That said, should you tire of endlessly meandering between beach and brunch, there's plenty to see and do elsewhere on the island – from strolling the streets of old Lahaina and biking down from the summit of Haleakalā to hiking alongside the waterfalls at ʻOheʻo Gulch or shopping for Hawaiian music.

◄ Windsurfing at Hoʻokipa

Maui
AT A GLANCE

UPCOUNTRY MAUI

Upcountry Maui, on the lower, western slopes of Haleakalā, is an unexpected idyll, its cool green meadows and flower farms offering a pastoral escape from the bustle below.

◄ ʻĪao Valley

◄ Upcountry Maui

THE CENTRAL ISTHMUS

The "neck" that connects Maui's two volcanoes is home to Kahului, the main commercial center; Pāʻia, a former plantation community turned surf-bum hang-out; and the faded but somehow appealing town of Wailuku, standing guard over the once-sacred ʻĪao Valley.

SOUTH MAUI

According to the far from instinctive local usage, "South Maui" refers to the coastal resorts of Kīhei, Wailea and Mākena, along the southwest shoreline of eastern Maui. The further south you go here, the better the beaches you'll find.

South Maui beach ▶

◄ Lahaina Harbor

HALEAKALĀ CRATER

Climb above the clouds to look out across the many-hued volcanic wasteland of vast Haleakalā Crater, or dwindle into cosmic insignificance as you hike down into it.

► Haleakalā Crater

LAHAINA

Once the capital of Hawaii and the rendezvous for the wild-living Pacific whaling fleet, Lahaina is the best place to get a sense of Maui's history.

THE ROAD TO HĀNA

The countless waterfalls and ravines that line the tortuous, demanding road to Hāna, on the windward coasts of eastern Maui, make for a wonderful day-trip, culminating at lush 'Ohe'o Gulch.

◄ The road to Hāna

Ideas

The big six

You'd have to stay on Maui a very long time to sample everything the island has to offer. As well as all that stupendous Polynesian scenery, it boasts superb tourist facilities, catering to every imaginable need and offering an extraordinary range of activities and opportunities. The sheer beauty of the place is probably what will stay with you the longest; but if you're lucky enough to see a whale breaching, that may blot out everything else.

▲ The Road to Hanā

However long you're going to spend on Maui, set aside at least a day to explore the island's wetter eastern shoreline; the scenery is out of this world.

P.126 ▸ ROAD TO HĀNA

▲ Haleakalā Crater

Large enough to hold all Manhattan, what the ancient Hawaiians called "the House of the Sun" offers a spectacle of extraordinary desolation and beauty.

P.115 ▸ HALEAKALĀ

◀ Surfing

Even if you don't learn the noble art of surfing while you're visiting its original home, you'll be not be able to resist seeing how it's done.

P.128 ▸ ROAD TO HĀNA

▶ The Feast at Lele

Forget the *lū'aus*; pay a little extra, and enjoy some truly great food while you watch top-notch *hula* performers.

P.58 ▸ LAHAINA

▼ Big Beach

Everyone's fantasy of the perfect Hawaiian beach; a huge stretch of golden sand pounded by awesome Pacific surf.

P.101 ▸ WAILEA AND MĀKENA

◀ Whales

No matter how often you see them – and you will, if you're here in winter – Maui's humpbacks remain utterly breathtaking.

P.54 ▸ LAHAINA

Scenic spots

Above all else, Maui is a natural wonderland, with magnificent landscapes on every side of the island as well, of course, as right on top. The finest scenery of all tends to be in areas where the rainfall is heavy enough to support rich green vegetation, which means you may well have to drive from your dry, sunny hotel to see it – but you certainly won't regret it.

▲ 'Īao Valley

Beautiful 'Īao Valley is the highlight of any tour of central Maui.

P.84 ▶ CENTRAL MAUI

▲ Haleakalā Crater

Hike into this extraordinary moonscape of craters and cinder cones at the top of Maui, and you're a world away from the beaches and resorts below.

P.115 ▶ HALEAKALĀ

▲ Kahakuloa Head

This towering highlight of the little-known Kahekili Highway guards a lovely traditional village.

P.69 ▸ NORTHWEST MAUI

▼ 'Ohe'o Gulch

Still widely – and spuriously – known as the Seven Sacred Pools, this tumbling sequence of waterfalls offers some great hiking.

P.142 ▸ BEYOND HĀNA

◀ Wai'ānapanapa State Park

For coastal hiking, camping, and even cave-exploring, this gorgeous park in East Maui has no rival.

P.133 ▸ THE ROAD TO HĀNA

▼ Ke'anae Peninsula

There can only be one winner where the full force of the Pacific crashes endlessly against the palm-studded black lava of the Ke'anae Peninsula; and it's not the island.

P.130 ▸ THE ROAD TO HĀNA

Beaches

There are enough good beaches all over Maui that you shouldn't have to stray more than a mile or two from your accommodation in order to find one. Even so, half the fun of visiting is to keep searching for the "perfect" stretch of sand; and with so many to choose from, the quest is likely to be unending. In terms of areas, the shorelines of West and South Maui hold the best beaches – and by no coincidence, that's where nearly all the hotels are.

▲ Red Sand Beach

A short but dangerous hike leads to a genuine curio, a "pocket beach" of volcanic red sand that has its own strange beauty.

P.137 ▶ THE ROAD TO HĀNA

▼ Kā'anapali Beach

Perhaps the best family beach on Maui, this lovely golden strand stretches right in front of the hotels, restaurants, and stores of upscale Kā'anapali.

P.61 ▶ KĀ'ANAPALI

▲ Polo Beach

Though it's dominated by mighty resort hotels, this is still unquestionably Wailea's finest beach, drawing daily crowds from all over the island.

P.100 ▸ WAILEA AND MĀKENA

▲ Maluaka Beach

One of the loveliest spots to watch the sunset on Maui, and a great place to swim and snorkel, especially if you're staying at the adjacent *Maui Prince*.

P.101 ▸ WAILEA AND MĀKENA

▲ Big Beach

Though the mighty waves that slam this magnificent expanse of sand make swimming dangerous, strolling is idyllic, and boogie-boarding, for experts at least, is irresistible.

P.101 ▸ WAILEA AND MĀKENA

▼ Wai'ānapanapa Beach

Close to Hāna in remote East Maui, this gorgeous black-sand beach makes a superb spectacle, fringed with lush green palms and washed with white surf.

P.133 ▸ THE ROAD TO HĀNA

Surfing and windsurfing

Maui holds some of the best surfing and windsurfing beaches in the world. However, anyone new to Hawaii, no matter how experienced elsewhere, should be sure to acclimatize at a few of the "lesser" spots before graduating to the challenging conditions of legendary places like Honolua Bay or Ho'okipa Beach. If you're looking to learn to surf or windsurf, then take lessons with a local; the gentle surf of Lahaina or Kīhei is ideal for beginners.

▲ Honomanū Bay

Fronted by a black-sand beach, this lush bay on the Road to Hāna offers excellent surfing for those familiar with local conditions.

P.129 ▸ THE ROAD TO HĀNA

▲ Mā'alaea Bay

This huge curving bay, protected by two volcanoes yet open to the Pacific winds, makes a wonderful playground for windsurfers from around the globe.

P.86 ▸ CENTRAL MAUI

▶ Honolua Bay

At the northern tip of West Maui, the island's most popular destination for serious surfers makes a lovely setting even if you're only going to watch.

P.67 ▶ NORTH-WEST MAUI

▼ Jaws

The supreme challenge for surfers; to get here at all you'll have to tackle several miles of red-dirt road, while to do battle with its stupendous waves takes a jet-ski tow-in.

P.128 ▶ THE ROAD TO HĀNA

▼ Kanahā Beach

The best place to learn to windsurf on Maui, this beach throngs daily with eager sail-boarding students keen to move on to awesome Ho'okipa.

P.74 ▶ KAHULUI

▲ Ho'okipa Beach

Commonly acknowledged as the world's best windsurfing spot, this central beach park plays host to major championships, and is also used by regular surfers.

P.126 ▶ THE ROAD TO HĀNA

Historic Maui

Maui's latest incarnation as a vacation playground is a recent development. The history of the island goes back a lot farther than that; some of the temples where ancient Hawaiians performed human sacrifices are still standing, while the nineteenth-century homes of missionaries and whaling captains give towns like Lahaina and Wailuku an added charm. You'll also come to realize how plantation laborers from all over the world gave modern Hawaii its cosmopolitan character.

ALEXANDER & BALDWIN
SUGAR
MUSEUM

▲ Hanā

Slow down your pace to enjoy a day or two in time-forgotten Hanā, a relic of how all Maui must have been before the advent of tourism.

P.134 ▸ THE ROAD TO HĀNA

▲ Piʻilanihale Heiau

What may well be the largest ancient Polynesian temple ever constructed, anywhere, stands in beautiful oceanfront gardens not far from Hanā.

P.132 ▸ THE ROAD TO HĀNA

▲ Alexander & Baldwin Sugar Museum

Learn about the nineteenth-century heyday of the sugar industry, and how immigrant laborers from all over the world combined to forge Maui's modern identity.

P.75 ▸ KAHULUI

▶ The Bailey House

The best historical museum on the island focuses on the coming of the first Christian missionaries, but also reflects the heritage of the ancient Hawaiians.

P.78 ▸ WAILUKU

▼ Lahaina

Once the capital of the Kingdom of Hawaii, and later a haven for roistering whaling crews, Lahaina remains Maui's prettiest old town, and still holds some lovely nineteenth-century buildings.

P.49 ▸ LAHAINA

Resort hotels

Maui and Lanai hold some of the world's most luxurious hotels. Enclaves like Kapalua and Kā'anapali in West Maui, and Wailea and Mākena in South Maui can boast some truly extraordinary self-contained resorts, where sky-high room rates give guests access to utter luxury. Mere mortals can always venture in to dine at the restaurants and use other facilities, however, and no resort can stop outsiders from visiting the invariably superb adjoining beaches.

▲ Four Seasons Resort Lanai at Mānele Bay

The quintessential Hawaiian resort hotel stands above the best beach on the so-called "private island" of Lanai.

P.165 ▸ ACCOMMODATION

▼ Four Seasons Resort Maui at Wailea

Smart, elegant resort that's home to some great restaurants and amenities, and is right by a lovely beach.

P.163 ▸ ACCOMMODATION

▶ Hotel Hanā-Maui

Luxurious individual "cottages" are
scattered across lawns that slope
down the East Maui shoreline, facing
the sunrise from the unspoiled town
of Hanā.

P.165 ▸ ACCOMMODATION

◀ Fairmont Kea Lani

Topped by gleaming white Moorish domes,
the *Fairmont Kea Lani* is a true fantasy-land
where you feel your every wish will be
granted.

P.162 ▸ ACCOMMODATION

▼ Hyatt Regency

With its waterslides and lagoons, and beachfront location, Kāʻanapali's finest resort hotel
is an opulent playground.

P.158 ▸ ACCOMMODATION

▶ Maui Prince

Mākena's only hotel enjoys a great
oceanfront setting, with a splendid
little beach and wonderful sunset
views of Molokini.

P.163 ▸ ACCOMMODATION

Affordable accommodation

Visiting Maui doesn't have to cost the earth; genuinely affordable options can be found even in the major resort areas. The inns and hotels spotlighted here are by no means the cheapest of them all, but they're well-priced places that offer genuine charm and value. If you're looking for an intimate getaway, it's worth considering Maui's B&Bs, which can be far more romantic than a hotel. And for travelers on a restricted budget, the island also holds a handful of hostels.

▲ Old Wailuku Inn

Lovely historic home in Wailuku, handy for everywhere, with classy guest suites, tasteful furnishings, and a friendly feel.

P.161 ▸ ACCOMMODATION

▲ Old Lahaina House

Very friendly B&B close to the heart of Lahaina, which offers bright rooms and even has its own pool.

P.158 ▸ ACCOMMODATION

▼ Hotel Lanai

Although the island of Lanai is justly renowned as an expensive destination, this charming plantation-era hotel offers old-fashioned comfort at old-fashioned prices.

▲ Banana Bungalow

Popular with international travelers, Wailuku's *Banana Bungalow* makes a great central base for cost-conscious visitors – they often offer free island excursions.

▶ Hāmoa Bay House and Bungalow

An utterly idyllic honeymoon hideaway, engulfed in the lush rainforest of East Maui.

▼ The Mauian

Good rooms at great prices, right next to gorgeous Nāpili Beach in a friendly family-run atmosphere – what more could you want?

Hikes

Maui may not look that big on the map, and in places it can feel too over-developed for comfort, but there's still plenty of unspoiled wilderness out there if you're prepared to strap on a pair of hiking boots and leave the highway behind. Haleakalā is the ultimate test, but be sure also to take a hike into the rainforest at some point. Although East Maui is the obvious destination, the valleys and hillsides of West Maui also hold some fabulous trails, within very easy reach of the resorts.

▼ 'Ula'ino Road

Short, easy coastal hike that leads to a ravishing oceanfront waterfall-cum-grotto known as the "Blue Pool".

P.132 ▸ THE ROAD TO HĀNA

▼ Sliding Sands Trail

It takes commitment and stamina to hike this grueling high-altitude trail, but you won't soon forget its close-up views of the wonders of Haleakalā Crater.

P.120 ▸ HALEAKALĀ

▲ Waihe'e Ridge Trail

Climb as high as it's possible to go into the mountains of West Maui, to see lost swamps, uninhabited valleys, and breathtaking wild orchids.

P.80 ▸ WAILUKU

▶ Pīpīwai Trail

This fabulous rainforest hike passes through an eerie, dark bamboo grove en route to a remote waterfall high in Kīpahulu Valley.

P.143 ▸ BEYOND HĀNA

▼ Waikamoi Nature Trail

Escape the crowds on the legendary Road to Hanā by taking this tranquil little trail into the forests.

P.128 ▸ THE ROAD TO HĀNA

Tours and excursions

With so much of Maui to see, if you restrict yourself to places you can reach in your own vehicle you're likely to miss out on some of its most exciting attractions. Taking a helicopter trip is very highly recommended indeed, for a literal overview of the island, while it's also well worth taking a boat trip to see whales, to snorkel at little Molokini, or to cross over to neighboring Lanai. A guided bus tour isn't a bad idea even if you've rented a car; you might actually get to see more than the road ahead.

▲ Lanai

Explore the so-called "private island" of Lanai on an eight-mile ferry trip from Lahaina.

P.147 ▸ LANAI

▼ Helicopter flight

Get a bird's eye view of the whole island – you can even fly right over the top of Haleakalā – and you'll see enough beauty spots to keep you busy for the rest of your trip.

P.174 ▸ ESSENTIALS

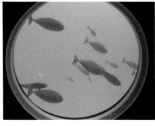

▲ Atlantis submarines

Non-divers can admire Hawaii's wondrous marine life from the cabin of a real-life yellow submarine.

P.177 ▸ ESSENTIALS

▼ Molokini

This tiny volcanic remnant, poking from the Pacific off South Maui, makes a great destination for snorkeling or diving cruises.

P.177 ▸ ESSENTIALS

▲ Whale watching

In winter, the waters off Maui are alive with frolicking humpback whales; watch them from the beach, or take a cruise to see them up close.

P.54 ▸ LAHAINA

▼ Bus tour to Hanā

Letting someone else handle the twists and turns of driving the famed Road to Hanā leaves you free to enjoy the sumptuous scenery.

P.126 ▸ THE ROAD TO HĀNA

Maui for kids

If the weather stays fine for your whole vacation, then you shouldn't find much trouble keeping the kids happy. Quite apart from the various activities and beaches listed elsewhere in this book, however, Maui does also hold some fun attractions for kids, with the aquarium at the Maui Ocean Center top among them.

▲ Waterslides

What child could resist the intricate labyrinths of tunnels and waterslides to be found at hotels like Kā'anapali's *Westin Maui*?

P.159 ▸ ACCOMMODATION

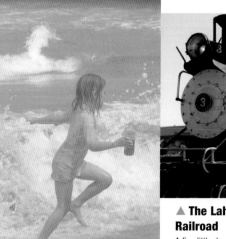

▲ The Lahaina Kā'anapali Railroad

A fine little day-trip in West Maui; ride the plantation railroad from historic Lahaina to the beach at Kā'anapali.

P.174 ▸ ESSENTIALS

▲ Whale Museum

This little museum, perched above the stores in central Kāʻanapali, brings the fascinating world of the whalers to life.

P.62 ▸ KĀʻANAPALI

◀ Kāʻanapali Beach

Pretty much any beach on Maui will delight the kids, but Kāʻanapali is probably the best, for convenience and safety as well as soft sand.

P.61 ▸ KĀʻANAPALI

▼ Maui Ocean Center

This top-quality aquarium is the perfect rainy-day destination, providing a chance to learn all about the colorful denizens of the Hawaiian deep.

P.86 ▸ CENTRAL MAUI

Gourmet restaurants

Maui is blessed with an abundance of truly excellent restaurants; choosing just five feels like skimming the surface. The most distinctive feature of island cuisine has been the emergence of something loosely known as "Hawaiian Regional" or "new Hawaiian" food, which closely resembles what may be familiar as Pacific Rim cooking. Features include cooking fresh fish to accentuate its delicate flavors, and complementing dishes with Asian herbs and spices.

▲ Roy's

Roy Yamaguchi is a pioneer of modern Hawaiian cooking; both his Maui restaurants, at Kahana and Kīhei, serve truly delicious food.

P.70 & P.96 ▸ NORTHWEST MAUI & KĪHEI

▲ Kaʻuiki

The atmospheric terrace setting and laid-back ambience of the dining room at the *Hotel Hanā-Maui* is matched by the excellence of its inventive Pacific-Rim cuisine.

P.138 ▸ THE ROAD TO HĀNA

▲ Haili'imaile General Store

Far from the resorts, and housed in a former grocery store, this Upcountry restaurant thrives on the reputation of a great and ever-changing Asian-flavored menu.

P.113 ▸ UPCOUNTRY MAUI

▲ Sansei

With two locations, in Kapalua and Kīhei, *Sansei* serves up the best Japanese-style fish on the island, at surprisingly reasonable prices.

P.70 & P.96 ▸ NORTHWEST MAUI & KĪHEI

◀ Spago

In this ultra-glamorous resort restaurant, beautifully poised at Wailea's Four Seasons, Wolfgang Puck pulls out all the stops to deliver superb Pacific-Rim dishes.

P.106 ▸ WAILEA AND MĀKENA

Casual eating

Not every meal on Maui can be a gourmet extravaganza; you'll also find plenty of straightforward restaurants that serve good food at affordable prices. Enough tourists are out exploring the island every day that high-quality cafés flourish almost everywhere, while all the fresh fruit and other island produce means that even roadside stalls offer surprisingly tasty snacks to passing travelers.

▼ Penne Pasta

This popular, ever-expanding pizza and pasta joint offers Lahaina's best value for a tasty meal.

P.59 ▶ LAHAINA

▼ Soup Nutz and Java Jazz

Funky, friendly cafe in West Maui; relax over an early coffee, or enjoy some jazz in the evening.

P.71 ▶ NORTHWEST MAUI

▲ Cilantro Fresh Mexican Grill

Top-notch, and unusually healthy, Mexican fast food in the heart of Lahaina.

P.57 ▸ LAHAINA

◀ AK's Cafe

Good, healthy food in Central Maui; a convenient stop-off for a quick meal as you tour the island.

P.82 ▸ WAILUKU

▼ Nāhiku Fruit Stand

One of the true highlights along the Road to Hanā; delicious juices, smoothies and snacks, with an excellent barbecue place alongside.

P.139 ▸ THE ROAD TO HĀNA

Hawaiian food and drink

Although it has to be acknowledged that because Hawaii belongs to the United States, you can get pretty much any fast food on Maui that you'd expect to find on the mainland US, there's still plenty that's distinctively Hawaiian. The best place to sample traditional foods like *kālua* pork is at a commercial *lū'au*, while the favorite dishes introduced to the island by generations of immigrants features on the menus of "local" diners all over Maui.

▲ Cocktails

Why come all the way to Hawaii unless it's to drink a Mai Tai at sunset with a paper parasol poking from the glass?

P.106 ▶ WAILEA AND MĀKENA

▼ Fruit stands

Maui's abundance of succulent fresh fruit means that roadside shacks practically give the stuff away.

P.139 ▶ THE ROAD TO HĀNA

▼ Fish in a fancy restaurant

The chefs of Maui are renowned for their inventive ways with fish; be sure to try *opah* (moonfish) or *moi* (threadfish) at one of the island's top restaurants.

P.63 ▶ KĀ'ANAPALI

▲ Saimin

If Hawaii has a national dish these days, it's *saimin*, or noodle soup; you can buy a bowl for under $5 in cafes all over the island.

P.114 ▶ UPCOUNTRY MAUI

▼ Poi

The authentic taste of old Hawaii; you have to try this purple taro-root paste at least once, even if you end up agreeing with Captain Cook that it's a "disagreeable mess."

P.173 ▶ ESSENTIALS

▶ Kālua pork at a lū'au

Baked all day in an underground oven, shredded *kālua* pork, reminiscent of Southern barbecued hog, is a highlight of Maui's *lūaus*.

P.58 ▶ LAHAINA

Flora and fauna

Hawaii is an extraordinary ecological laboratory. Not only are the islands isolated by a "moat" at least two thousand miles wide in every direction, but, having emerged from the sea as lifeless lumps of lava, they were never populated by the diversity of species that spread across the rest of the planet. That means Maui is still home to its own unique ecosystem, featuring plants, birds, and insects found nowhere else on earth.

▲ Birds

Maui is home to some of the rarest birds on the planet, with differing habitats that support an extraordinary range of species.

P.129 ▸ THE ROAD TO HĀNA

▲ Silverswords

The rare and delicate silversword plant, found only on the highest slopes of Hawaii's volcanoes, makes a ravishing spectacle even if you don't get to see its once-in-a-lifetime flowering.

P.124 ▸ HALEAKALĀ

▶ Orchids

Whether growing wild in remote valleys and hillsides, or carefully cultivated in commercial gardens, Maui's iridescent orchids are an unfailing delight.

P.126 ▶ THE ROAD TO HĀNA

▲ The rainforest

Even if you spend most of your vacation in the sun, be sure to venture down at least one of the many trails that penetrate the lush heart of Maui's rainforest.

P.142 ▶ BEYOND HĀNA

▼ Protea

The farms of Upcountry Maui are renowned for their multi-colored protea blooms, a perfect touch of color to take home.

P.107 ▶ UPCOUNTRY MAUI

▼ Gardens

Gardens all over the island are open to the public, giving visitors the chance to see and buy blossoms seldom encountered in the wild.

P.109 ▶ UPCOUNTRY MAUI

Shows and nightlife

Maui's nightlife, it has to be admitted, is relatively sedate; there just doesn't seem to be a large enough local population for clubs or other nightspots to cater to a regular clientele. Instead, most of the entertainment on offer is firmly directed at tourists, and often panders to preconceptions of what Polynesia "ought" to be like rather than how Hawaii actually is. That said, *lūʻaus* can be great fun even if they're not "authentic," and with luck you'll get to hear some great Hawaiian music too.

▲ Drums of the Pacific

If Hawaiian-style entertainment is more important to you than the food, you'll enjoy the show at this Kāʻanapali *lūʻau*.

P.64 ▸ KĀʻANAPALI

▲ The Feast at Lele

A fantastic setting, superb and unusual food, and a great show – not a *lūʻau* exactly, but the best night out on Maui.

P.58 ▸ LAHAINA

▶ Slack key night

Superb Hawaiian music, performed by the very top masters of the genre in a setting that's transformed by the joy of artists and audience alike.

P.71 ▶ NORTHWEST MAUI

▼ Maui Sunset Lūʻau

The best *lūʻau* in South Maui, with lovely views out to Molokini and an entertaining family show.

P.106 ▶ WAILEA AND MĀKENA

▶ Old Lahaina Lūʻau

The island's finest *lūʻau*, in a spacious oceanfront location in Lahaina, and offering an authentic taste of traditional Hawaiian hula.

P.60 ▶ LAHAINA

Ocean fun

The scope for enjoying yourself in the sea off Maui is virtually infinite. Take some basic precautions, like informing yourself of local beach conditions – ask a lifeguard, or someone at your hotel, or read this book – protect yourself against the sun, and get on with it. Surfing and windsurfing are summarized on p.174, but there are plenty of activities that don't require that level of expertise.

▲ Boogie-boarding

Much of the thrill of surfing, with little of the effort; many resort beaches offer ideal conditions for first-time boogie-boarders.

P.101 ▶ WAILEA AND MĀKENA

▼ Diving

Hawaii's warm Pacific waters are home to swarms of colorful fish, making Maui a paradise for divers.

P.176 ▶ ESSENTIALS

▶ Swimming

You don't need a reservation, you don't need fancy equipment, and you don't have to pay anyone; just get in the water and get on with it.

P.98 ▶ WAILEA AND MĀKENA

▲ Snorkeling

Exploring the nooks and crannies of Maui's coast with a mask and fins can be endlessly fascinating.

P.61 ▶ KĀ'ANAPALI

▼ Kayaking

Ocean kayaking, especially along the shorelines of South and West Maui, is rewarding and exhilarating.

P.103 ▶ WAILEA AND MĀKENA

Outdoor activities

Think of something you like doing outdoors, and you can bet someone on Maui has set up a business that will let you do it (well, maybe not that). Maui is renowned among the Hawaiian islands as attracting the most active visitors – the ones who want to ride things, jump off things, and generally rush around enjoying themselves – and you'll be given every opportunity to join in.

▼ Downhill biking

The ultimate in leisure travel; after being driven to the top of Haleakalā at dawn, you simply roll back down again from the park entrance, and barely have to nudge a pedal for thirty miles.

P.115 ▶ HALEAKALĀ

▼ Skyline

An adventurous option in the Upcountry woodlands – a daredevil course of aerial ziplines.

P.110 ▶ UPCOUNTRY MAUI

▲ Paragliding

Get even closer to heaven by soaring on the thermal air currents above beautiful Upcountry Maui.

P.109 ▶ UPCOUNTRY MAUI

◀ Golf

Maui's meticulously groomed resort golf courses are among the very finest on the planet.

P.180 ▶ ESSENTIALS

▼ Horse riding

Opportunities for horse riding can be found all over Maui, from guided trips through Haleakalā Crater to galloping through remote meadows.

P.179 ▶ ESSENTIALS

Shopping and souvenirs

While not on par with Honolulu as a shopping destination, Maui does hold plenty of malls, stores, and shopping streets. As well as all those ephemeral needs you suddenly encounter on a tropical holiday – sunhats, swimming costumes, aloha shirts – it also offers abundant souvenirs to show the folks back home what they were missing. And some of the crafts are even worth buying for yourself.

▲ Tiki products

You'll be needing a few *hula* dolls, *tiki* carvings and cocktail accessories for that Hawaiian theme bar you're going to build in your basement.

P.88 ▸ CENTRAL MAUI

▲ Hula crafts

If you want to buy something truly Hawaiian, how about the various artefacts you'll see used in *hula* performances, like a decorated gourd or a feathered rattle?

P.88 ▸ CENTRAL MAUI

▶ Lau hala weaving

This distinctive Hawaiian craft, using woven palm leaves, creates some wonderful souvenirs.

P.88 ▸ CENTRAL MAUI

▲ Leis

You'll know you're in Hawaii when you're garlanded with your first lei; why not take one home to your friends and family?

P.182 ▸ ESSENTIALS

▼ Aloha wear

Yes, everyone really does wear Hawaiian shirts in Hawaii; and before you know it you'll find yourself wearing one too.

P.81 ▸ WAILUKU

▼ Hawaiian Music

Few first-time visitors leave Maui without a new-found love for Hawaiian music; be sure to pick up that Israel Kamakawiwo'ole or Hapa CD while you still can.

P.94 ▸ KĪHEI

Places

Lahaina

Lahaina, the only true town in West Maui, is one of the prettiest communities in all Hawaii. Timber-frame buildings line its main oceanfront street; yachts bob in the harbor; coconut palms sway to either side of the central banyan tree; surfers swirl into the thin fringe of beach to the south; and the mountains of West Maui dominate the skyline. Lahaina is lively and by Maui standards inexpensive, with a huge range of activities and little rainfall, but above all it's the island's only town with lodging, sightseeing, nightlife, and an abundance of restaurants within easy walking distance of each other. At times it can be unpleasantly crowded, but even so Lahaina is unquestionably an attractive base. Early evening is especially unforgettable, with the sun casting a rich glow on the mountains as it sets behind the island of Lanai.

Banyan Tree Square

At the very heart of Lahaina, Banyan Tree Square is an attractive public space that's often rendered a little too busy for comfort by large influxes of tourists. The magnificent banyan tree that almost completely fills it was planted in 1873, and consists of at least twenty major trunks. Chirruping birds congregate in the branches, while portrait artists tout for customers in the shade below.

Here and there on the surrounding lawns, outlines mark the former extent of Lahaina Fort, built in 1832 and demolished in 1854. One small corner of its walls, which once held 47 cannons, has been reconstructed, at the southwest end of the square.

The Court House

The stolid, four-square Court House, on the harbor side of the square, dates from 1859. Downstairs, you'll find the small local visitor center (see p.169), as well as the Banyan Tree Gallery, which hosts interesting free art exhibitions (daily 9am–5pm). Up on the second floor, the town's former courtroom, last used in 1987, now serves as the Lahaina

Some history

There's little left to show for it nowadays, but Lahaina boasts a colorful past. Kamehameha the Great spent a year here preparing for what was to be an unsuccessful invasion of Kauai, while his successors, Kamehamehas II and III, ruled from Lahaina between the 1820s and 1840s. Hard-bitten whaling crews jostled with missionaries in a rip-roaring frontier town once described as "one of the breathing holes of Hell." Lahaina spent most of the twentieth century as a sleepy sugar town – its mill eventually closed in 1999 – and only turned into the hectic tourist destination of today after the emergence of the resort development at neighboring Kā'anapali during the 1970s.

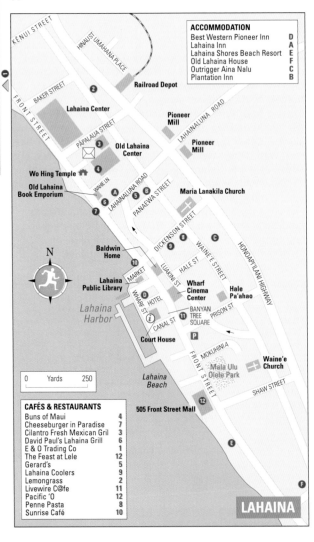

ACCOMMODATION

Best Western Pioneer Inn	D
Lahaina Inn	A
Lahaina Shores Beach Resort	E
Old Lahaina House	F
Outrigger Aina Nalu	C
Plantation Inn	B

Railroad Depot

Lahaina Center

Pioneer Mill

Pioneer Mill

Old Lahaina Center

Wo Hing Temple

Old Lahaina Book Emporium

Maria Lanakila Church

Baldwin Home

N

Lahaina Public Library

Lahaina Harbor

Wharf Cinema Center

Hale Pa'ahao

Court House

BANYAN TREE SQUARE

Lahaina Beach

Waine'e Church

Mala Ulu Olele Park

505 Front Street Mall

0   Yards   250

CAFÉS & RESTAURANTS

Buns of Maui	4
Cheeseburger in Paradise	7
Cilantro Fresh Mexican Gril	3
David Paul's Lahaina Grill	6
E & O Trading Co	1
The Feast at Lele	12
Gerard's	5
Lahaina Coolers	9
Lemongrass	2
Livewire C@fe	11
Pacific 'O	12
Penne Pasta	8
Sunrise Café	10

LAHAINA

Heritage Center (same hours; $2 suggested donation), where displays on local history focus especially on the whaling era.

The Pioneer Inn

Across Hotel Street from the Court House, the *Pioneer Inn* has, since it was moved from Lanai in 1901, been the main social center of Lahaina. Its original owner, a Canadian "Mountie" who had pursued a criminal all the way to Maui, decided to stay on and go into the hotel business. Still a hotel – see p.157 – it makes an atmospheric place to stop in for a beer.

The Brick Palace and the Hauola Stone

The Lahaina Public Library stands on the site of a royal taro patch, personally tended by the first three Kamehamehas. Bricks set into the grass on its seaward side trace the foundations of the Brick Palace, Hawaii's first Western-style building, which was built for Kamehameha the Great in 1798 by an English convict who had managed to escape from Australia.

Poking out from the waves beyond the seawall to the north, the approximately chair-shaped Hauola Stone was a "healing rock" where Hawaiian women would give birth. In thanks for a trouble-free labor, the umbilical cord of the infant would be left under the rock.

Lahaina Harbor

On the waterfront, across from the *Pioneer Inn*, a simple, modern white structure has replaced what was the oldest Pacific Lighthouse, built to serve the whaling fleet in 1840. Shielded by a breakwater of boulders, Lahaina Harbor now serves as an overworked pleasure-boat marina, and is also the base for

ferries to Lanai (see p.170) and Molokai. Although the harbor wall has kiosks for most local boat operators, it's not much of an area to stroll around, and you can usually get better prices for trips from the activity centers along Front Street.

Lahaina Beach

Immediately south of the marina, Lahaina Beach, with its shallow water, sandy bottom, and gentle breaks, is where companies such as the Goofy Foot Surf School (☎808/244-9283, ⓦwww .goofyfootsurfschool.com) and the Nancy Emerson School of Surfing (☎808/244-7873, ⓦwww.surfclinicsmaui.com) teach their clients the rudiments of surfing, and beginners and old-timers alike swoop back and forth. The beach itself is too narrow for long days of family fun, but it's fine for a stroll.

The Baldwin Home

The Baldwin Home, on Front Street just north of Banyan Tree Square, is Lahaina's oldest surviving building. Dating from the days when this was Hawaii's royal capital, it was the Maui base of the Sandwich

▲ LAHAINA HARBOR

Islands Mission and is now a reasonably interesting museum of missionary and local history (daily 10am–4pm; $3, $5 per couple or family; ☏808/661-3262). The admission price includes a brief narrated tour, after which visitors are free to take a closer look around.

Constructed in 1834, with 24-inch-thick walls of plastered lava and coral, the house is named for Reverend Dwight Baldwin, who took it over three years later. Baldwin remained as pastor of Lahaina's Waine'e Church until 1871, and much of his original furniture is still in place. Oddly frivolous touches among the chairs, quilts, and memorabilia include an inlaid *koa* gaming table, and a tabletop croquet set. On one wall hangs a "Native Doctor's License" from 1865, with a scale of charges ranging from $50 down to $10, according to whether the patient had a "Very great sickness," "Less than that," "A good deal less," a "Small sickness," or a "Very small."

Wo Hing Temple

The distinguished-looking building with the unmistakably Oriental facade, a short walk north along Front Street, is known as the Wo Hing Temple (daily 10am–4pm; $1). It was built in 1912 as the meeting place for the Wo Hing Society, a mutual-aid organization established in China during the seventeenth century. Until the 1970s it housed elderly members of the society, but it's now an intriguing little museum devoted to the Chinese immigration to Hawaii, with a small Taoist altar on its second story.

Amid the faded signs and battered pots and pans in the

▲ WO HING TEMPLE

decrepit adjacent cookhouse, you can watch scratchy film footage shot by Thomas Edison in Hawaii in 1898 and 1906. Shown in a continuous loop, it offers fascinating glimpses of Waikīkī before the tourists arrive, and plantation life before trucks replaced horses.

Waine'e Church

The first church on Maui, built in 1828 after five years of open-air services, was Waine'e Church, one block back from the sea. Twice destroyed by hurricanes, and burned down in 1894 during protests against the overthrow of the Hawaiian monarchy, this less-than-enthralling edifice has been officially known as Waiola Church since it was last rebuilt in 1953.

Tombs in the sun-scorched graveyard alongside, however,

include some of the greatest names in early Hawaiian history. A simple monument commemorates the last king of Kauai, Kaumuali'i, who was buried here in 1825 after being kidnapped and forced to live out the rest of his life in exile. Nearby are Queen Keopuolani, one of the many wives of Kamehameha the Great, who was of such distinguished blood that her husband could only enter her presence naked on all fours; the governor of Maui, Hoapili Kane, who died in 1840; and his widow and successor Hoapili Wahine.

Lahainaluna

High above Lahaina town, reached by a winding two-mile climb up Lahainaluna Road past the Pioneer Sugar Mill, Lahainaluna Seminary was founded by American missionaries in 1831. Its goal was to teach Hawaiians to read and write, in the hope of producing future teachers and ministers. In 1850, the seminary passed into government control, and it eventually became Hawaii's most prestigious public high school. During the Gold Rush years many Californians sent their children here rather than risk the long journey East.

Visitors are welcome to take a look around the high school grounds; identify yourself at the gate first. The only building you can enter is the seminary's small printing house, Hale Pa'i (Mon–Fri by appointment only; free; ☏808/661-3262). Dating from 1837, it holds some of Hawaii's first printed books, as well as a replica of the press that produced them.

Among the seminary's earliest pupils were Hawaii's most famous native historians, Samuel Kamakau and David Malo. Malo had been brought up at the court of Kamehameha the Great on the Big Island and was 38 when he first came here. Although he became a Christian, and was a minister at the old village of Kalepolepo in what's now Kīhei, he was also a passionate defender of the rights of the Hawaiian people. Before he died in 1853, he asked to be buried "beyond the rising tide of the foreign invasion." His gravesite, above Lahainaluna at Pu'u Pa'upa'u, is marked with a huge letter "L" (for Lahainaluna) etched into the hillside and visible from all over Lahaina.

Launiupoko State Wayside Park

While always scenic, the beaches immediately south of Lahaina are not nearly as appealing as those to the north, consisting as a rule of narrow strips of sand deposited atop sharp black rocks. Three miles out, Launiupoko State Wayside Park makes an attractive picnic spot. Coconut palms lean out from the shoreline, while larger trees shade the tables on the lawn; the only snag is that it's very much in earshot of the highway. From the center of the park, boulder walls curve out to enclose a shallow artificial pool, suitable for small children, with two narrow outlets to the sea. South of that is a small beach of gritty sand, while to the north the lava rocks create a sea wall, alive with scuttling black crabs. The gentle surf here makes the offshore waters ideal for apprentice surfers. The park offers showers and rest rooms, but camping is forbidden.

Olowalu

There's little more to Olowalu, six miles south of Lahaina, than a tiny row of stores *mauka* (inland) of the highway, which includes the restaurant *Chez Paul*, reviewed on p.57. Although there's no public access to the ocean, you can take a short hike towards the mountains to a cluster of ancient petroglyphs. Head round to the left behind the stores and then continue inland, following the dirt road that starts immediately left of a water tower. After ten minutes' walk through the cane fields, you reach a cinder cone from which one side has sheared off, leaving a flat wall of red rock. Railings a few feet up the rock mark the site of the petroglyphs, but the stairs and walkways that once enabled visitors to climb up to them have largely vanished. So too have many of the petroglyphs, while others have been vandalized. However, you should still spot several wedge-shaped human figures etched into the rock, together with a sailing canoe or two, characterized by their "crab-claw" sails.

Ukemehame and Pāpalaua

South of Olowalu, the cane fields come to an end, and Hwy-30 skirts the shoreline only a few feet above sea level. It's possible to park just about anywhere, and during the winter whale-watching season that's exactly what people do – often with very little warning.

Ukemehame Beach County Park, three miles along, consists of a very small area of lawn between the highway and the ocean, with picnic tables and a couple of portable rest rooms, fringed by a small strip of sand. It's all a bit exposed to the road, as although lots of trees have been planted, they remain

The Olowalu Massacre

Olowalu was the site of the worst massacre in Hawaiian history, perpetrated by Captain Simon Metcalfe of the American merchant ship *Eleanora* in 1790. After Hawaiians had killed a member of his crew as they stole one of the ship's boats off East Maui, Metcalfe sailed for Olowalu, which he was told was the home of the chief culprit. Offering to continue trading, he lured more than two hundred canoes out to the *Eleanora*, then bombarded them with his seven cannons. More than a hundred Hawaiians died.

Captain Metcalfe's 18-year-old son, Thomas, was to pay for his father's sins. Metcalfe had previously antagonized a Big Island chief, Kameʻeiamoku, who vowed to kill the next white man he met. Ignorant of events at Olowalu, Thomas Metcalfe landed at Kawaihae on the Big Island a few days later and was killed when Kameʻeiamoku attacked his six-man schooner *Fair American*. Only Isaac Davis of its crew was spared, for putting up such valiant resistance.

When the *Eleanora* arrived at Kawaihae in search of the younger Metcalfe, first mate John Young was sent ashore to investigate. After Kamehameha the Great himself prevented Young from rejoining his vessel, Captain Metcalfe concluded that his envoy had been killed and sailed away. Davis and Young remained on the islands for the rest of their lives. They were responsible for teaching the Hawaiians to fight with muskets and cannons – the royal arsenal began with two guns seized from the *Fair American* – and personally directed Kamehameha's armies in major battles during his conquest of all the Hawaiian islands.

▲ LAHAINA PALI TRAIL

very short. By this point, the mountains that rise just inland of the road are much drier and barer than further north.

Pāpalaua State Wayside, leading south from Ukemehame, is a long dirt strip used as a parking lot, separated from the sand by a thin line of scrubby trees. Local surfers and snorkelers – snorkeling is best around the rocks beyond the south end of the beach – set up tents, but there are virtually no facilities.

Papawai Point

Immediately beyond Pāpalaua, the highway starts its climb over (and through) the headland of Papawai Point. The roadside lookout here, which commands views across to Kahoolawe, Lanai, and East Maui, makes one of Maui's best whale-watching sites, but it can also cause traffic congestion in winter. Mā'alaea (see p.86) and the isthmus lie less than two miles further on.

The Lahaina Pali Trail

Until the hard labor of convicts constructed the first road around the southern coast of West Maui in 1900, the only way to reach Lahaina via dry land was to follow the centuries-old *alaloa*, or "long road," across the mountains. A five-mile stretch is now open as the Lahaina Pali Trail – a grueling hike that climbs 1600 feet above sea level and, being situated at the dry, exposed southern tip of the island, is also a very hot one. Don't expect to penetrate the mysterious green heart of the interior; for that, the Waihe'e Ridge Trail (see p.80) is a better bet. Your rewards instead will be the sight of some ravishing upland meadows, carpeted with magnificent purple, yellow, and red flowers, and expansive views out to the islands of Lanai and Kahoolawe and down across the isthmus. You'll also get a close-up look at the turbines recently erected to convert the powerful winds into electricity.

Both ends of the trail are a long way from the nearest town, so you'll need a car to reach either trailhead. Unless you can arrange to be picked up at the far end, hiking its full length necessitates a ten-mile round trip. The path leaves Honoapi'ilani Highway from a parking lot

▲ OLD LAHAINA BOOK EMPORIUM

near the 11-mile marker at Ukemehame and rejoins it five miles south of Wailuku, via a dirt road immediately south of the off-white bridge that lies between its intersections with highways 31 (to Kīhei) and 380 (to Kahului).

Whichever end you start – the eastern slope is the steeper – you'll have at least a mile of stiff climbing before the trail levels out, still far below the mountain tops. The trail then meanders through successive gulches to cross Kealaloloa Ridge, with almost the only shade being provided by the occasional native dryland sandalwood tree.

Shops

Lahaina Cannery Mall

1221 Honoapi'ilani Hwy, Lahaina ☎808/661-5304, ⓦwww .lahainacannerymall.com. Daily 9.30am–9pm. As well as Long's Drugs and Safeways for staple supplies, this largely indoor mall, at the north end of Lahaina near Mala Wharf, offers a good food court, assorted souvenir stores and tacky T-shirt places, and retailers ranging from Honolua Surf Co to Borders Express.

Lahaina Center

900 Front St, Lahaina ☎808/667-9216, ⓦwww.lahainacenter.com. Daily 10am–9pm. Three blocks north of Banyan Tree Square, across from the ocean, the Lahaina Center mall has never quite filled up, but it does hold some large clothing outlets, including aloha-wear specialists Hilo Hattie as well as Banana Republic, and also features its own reproduction Hawaiian village, the Hale Kahiko, which stages hula shows and is open for explanatory tours (daily 9am–6pm).

Old Lahaina Book Emporium

834 Front St, Lahaina ☎808/661-1399. Despite the address, Maui's best used bookstore is actually tucked slightly back from Front Street, but it's well worth tracking down, for a great selection of Hawaii-related books and much more besides.

Cafés

Buns of Maui

878 Front St, Lahaina ☎808/661-5407. Daily 7.30am–8.30pm. Tucked away just behind Front Street, this appealing little bakery serves fresh pastries, muffins, and of

course sumptuous cinnamon buns in the morning, and switches to sandwiches later on. It doesn't have espresso coffee, but there's a *Starbucks* nearby.

Livewire C@fe

612 Front St, Lahaina ☎ 808/661-4213. Daily 6am–9pm. The staff can be a little ditzy, but this roomy, tidy café, just south of Banyan Tree Square, serves good coffees, snacks and smoothies, and makes a convenient place to hang out and check your email.

Restaurants

Cheeseburger in Paradise

811 Front St, Lahaina ☎ 808/661-4855. Daily 8am–midnight. Busy, crowded seafront restaurant, perched on stilts above the water. The great views, buzzing ambience, and seafaring bric-a-brac are more of a draw than the food, which is very much what the name suggests, though in addition to meaty $8–10 cheeseburgers they have fish sandwiches and tofu nut-burgers at similar prices. There's live music nightly.

Chez Paul

Olowalu Village, Olowalu ☎ 808/661-3843. Dinner only, with two seatings at 6.30pm and 8.30pm. Closed Sun. Incongruous and very expensive French bistro, set behind a pretty little brick wall just off the highway six miles south of Lahaina. Most of the appetizers cost at least $10, though there's caviar for $95, while entrees such as fish poached in champagne or Tahitian duck are well over $30.

Cilantro Fresh Mexican Grill

Old Lahaina Center, 170 Papalaua Ave, Lahaina ☎ 808/667-5444. Mon–Sat 11am–9pm, Sun 11am–8pm. Simple but clean and very appetizing Mexican diner, where you order at the counter in front of the open kitchen, season your meal with a wide range of sauces and condiments, and either take it away or eat on site with plastic utensils. The food is uniformly tasty and fresh, with enchiladas, burritos and so on for $7–13, whole rotisserie chickens for $15, and specials like a chicken or fish taco plate for just over $10. There's no liquor license, but you can bring a bottle from the nearby *Foodland* supermarket.

David Paul's Lahaina Grill

Lahaina Inn, 127 Lahainaluna Rd, Lahaina ☎ 808/667-5117. Daily 6–10pm. Upmarket, dinner-only restaurant serving some of Maui's finest Pacific Rim cuisine, just off Front Street in downtown Lahaina. The setting is slightly cramped and unatmospheric, but the food is excellent. Of the appetizers, try the superb Kona lobster crabcake ($18). Entrees

▼ DAVID PAUL'S LAHAINA GRILL

include rack of lamb flavored with coffee ($41), *kalua* duck ($32), and various fish dishes, while the fruity desserts are wonderful. A five-course tasting menu costs $76.

E&O Trading Co

Lahaina Cannery Mall, 1221 Honoapiilani Highway, Lahaina ☎808/667-1818. Daily 11am–10pm. This sophisticated, relaxing pan-Asian restaurant, part of a Californian/Hawaiian chain, occupies a large indoor and outdoor space on the inland side of a mall at the northern end of Lahaina. A lunch of pad Thai noodles, spicy fish, or a burger costs $10–15. The dinner menu is divided between "small plates" such as Thai ahi poke at $7–15, and larger $17–35 plates, like a whole fish, intended for sharing and way too big to eat on your own. The nan bread is nothing special, but on the whole the meat and fish dishes are nicely varied and flavored. Reserve

▼ THE FEAST AT LELE

early to dine in one of the three tent-like indoor "pavilions". Happy hour daily 4–6pm, live music Thurs & Fri 6–8pm.

The Feast at Lele

505 Front St, Lahaina ☎808/667-5353 or 1-866/244-5353, ☺www .feastatlele.com. April–Sept daily 6pm, Oct–March daily 5.30pm; schedule may vary. An inspired cross between a *lūʻau* and a gourmet restaurant that, for once, lavishes as much care on the food as on the entertainment. Among the Polynesian specialties are *kalua* pork from Hawaii, *fafa* (steamed chicken) and *eʻiota* (marinated raw fish) from Tahiti, and grilled fish in banana leaves from Samoa. Each of the excellent and unusual five courses consists of at least two dishes, while the very romantic beachfront setting has individual tables set out facing the ocean at sunset. Music and *hula* performances punctuate the evening, culminating in a Samoan fire dance. Though steep, the $105 adult charge includes unlimited cocktails and other beverages; for children, it's $75. Reservations are essential.

Gerard's

Plantation Inn, 174 Lahainaluna Rd, Lahaina ☎808/661-8939. Daily 6–9pm. This upscale dinner-only restaurant adds a Hawaiian twist to traditional French cuisine, to create a menu of appetizers ($12.50–25) such as snails with wild mushrooms or *foie gras* with truffles, and entrees (up to $40) like veal sweetbreads or *opakapaka* (snapper). Desserts include *profiteroles* and other classic pastries.

Lahaina Coolers

180 Dickenson St, Lahaina ☎808/661-7082. Daily 8am–2am. Central bistro serving eggy breakfasts for around

▲ PACIFIC 'O

$10, then lunch specials like *kalua* pig tacos for around $10, or the same extensive menu of salads, pastas, pizzas, tortillas, steaks, and fresh Hawaiian fish for lunch and dinner, with entrees priced at $17–22. A couple of blocks from the sea, but it's open and breezy, with a pleasant atmosphere. British readers will be pleased to hear they show live English soccer games.

Lemongrass

930 Waine'e St, Lahaina ☏ 808/667-6888. Bright little Vietnamese/Thai restaurant, behind the Lahaina Center. In addition to soups and noodle dishes such as beef *phó* ($7) and pad Thai with shrimp or chicken ($10), there's a full menu of meat and seafood entrees, including plenty of curries, almost all under $15.

Pacific 'O

505 Front St, Lahaina ☏ 808/667-4341. Attractive, oceanfront mall-restaurant serving Pacific Rim cuisine on a beach-level terrace with indoor dining above. The relatively simple lunch specials ($10–15) include a bleu burger, a chicken wrap, and delicious sesame fish. In the evening, try appetizers ($9–16) such as the shrimp won tons in Hawaiian salsa, and entrees like "Thai dye duck" – a coconut curry ($25) – or tempura blocks of fish ($30). For vegetarians, the "leaning tower of tofu" costs $13.50 at lunch, $26 for dinner. Leave room for the huge, delicious chocolate desserts. Live jazz Fri & Sat from 9pm.

Penne Pasta

180 Dickenson St, Lahaina ☏ 808/661-6633. Cheerful Italian café, with sidewalk and indoor seating, serving straightforward but tasty pastas, salads, and pizzas for under $10. The thin, crispy flatbread topped with olives, capers, basil, oregano, and roasted peppers is particularly good. Lunch is served on weekdays only.

Sunrise Café

693A Front St at Market St, Lahaina ☏ 808/661-8558. Small, laidback, and very central café-cum-restaurant, with outdoor seating beside its own tiny patch of beach. Coffees, smoothies, and full cooked breakfasts are served from dawn onwards, plus $6–9 sandwiches, plate lunches, and salads later on. No credit cards.

Shows

Old Lahaina Lū'au

Lahaina Cannery Mall, 1251 Front St, Lahaina ☎ 808/667-1998 or 1-800/248-5828, ⓦ www.oldlahainaluau .com. April–Sept daily 5.45pm, Oct–March daily 5.15pm; $89, ages 12 and under $59. Maui's best *lū'au* shows its rivals how a *lū'au* really should be done; if it's the food that appeals most to you, then choose the Feast at Lele over this, but here you'll get something closer to the full *lū'au* experience. The spacious oceanfront location is ideal, enabling guests to explore the various displays and crafts stalls and watch the sunset before they're seated to enjoy a full meal of traditional foods like *kālua* pork, *poi*, and *lau lau*. The evening culminates with a skillfully staged show that traces the history of *hula*. Ticket prices include an open cocktail bar.

'Ulalena

Lahaina Center, 900 Front St, Lahaina ☎ 808/661-9913 or 1-877/688-

▼ OLD LAHAINA LŪ'AU

4800, ⓦ www.ulalena.com. Tues–Sat 6.30pm; $50–70, under-13s $30. This colorful song-and-dance stage show, recounting Hawaiian history from ancient legends to the present day, features energetic and talented performers, stirring drum-based music, and fine costumes and effects. If that's the kind of thing you like back home, then no doubt you'll like it here too, but if for example you're only tempted to see it because you're interested in Hawaiian music and culture, you may well not find it satisfying.

Warren and Annabelle's Magic Show

Lahaina Center, 900 Front St, Lahaina ☎ 808/667-6244, ⓦ www .warrenandannabelles.com. Mon–Sat 5pm & 7.30pm; adults only, $50, or $82 with food and two cocktails, or $86 with dessert as well. Although there's nothing particularly Hawaiian about this entertaining magic show, for a fun night out it's unbeatable. Each group of guests must solve a puzzle to gain admission to the pre-show bar, where cocktails and a large selection of appetizers and desserts are served while an invisible pianist (the ghostly "Annabelle") plays show tunes. The whole audience then moves to the intimate showroom, where they're treated to a wonderful display of sleight-of-hand magic by Warren Gibson, many of whose tricks are truly mind-boggling. Note that the two shows overlap; the entire evening lasts four hours.

Kāʻanapali

When American Factors (Amfac), the owners of the Pioneer Sugar Mill, decided in 1957 to transform the oceanfront cane fields of Kāʻanapali into a luxury tourist resort, they established a pattern that has been repeated throughout Hawaii ever since. There had never been a town at Kāʻanapali, but there was a superb white-sand beach – far better than anything at Lahaina – backed by a tract of land that was ripe for development and more than twice the size of Waikīkī. The first hotel opened in 1963 and has been followed by half a dozen similar giants, whose four thousand rooms now welcome half a million visitors each year. There's still little else in Kāʻanapali apart from the anodyne Whalers Village mall, though. Kāʻanapali is a pretty enough place, with its palm-fringed beach, two rolling golf courses and sunset views of the island of Lanai filling the western horizon, but it's a little lacking in Hawaiian flavor.

Kāʻanapali Beach

Kāʻanapali Beach is divided into two separate long strands by the forbidding, three-hundred-foot cinder cone of Puʻu Kekaʻa, known as the Black Rock. The sand shelves away abruptly from both sections, so swimmers soon find themselves in deep water, but bathing is usually safe outside periods of high winter surf. The rugged lava coastline around the Black Rock itself, close to the *Sheraton* resort, is one of the best snorkeling spots on Maui.

As ever in Hawaii, where every beach is publicly owned, you don't have to be staying at one of Kāʻanapali's hotels to use the main beach, but there are also a couple of public beach parks just around the headland to the south. Both Hanakaʻōʻō and Wahikuli are right alongside Hwy-30; swimming is generally safer at Wahikuli, but the facilities and general ambience are more appealing at Hanakaʻōʻō.

▼ KĀʻANAPALI BEACH

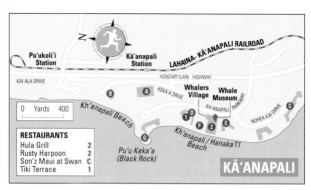

RESTAURANTS

Hula Grill	2
Rusty Harpoon	2
Son'z Maui at Swan	C
Tiki Terrace	1

ACCOMMODATION

Hyatt Regency Maui	C	Royal Lahaina Resort	B	The Whaler on	
Kā'anapali Beach Hotel	D	Sheraton Maui	G	Kā'anapali Beach	F
Outrigger Maui Eldorado	A	The Westin Maui	E		

Whale Museum

A pavilion at the main (inland) entrance to the Whalers Village mall shelters the articulated skeleton of a sperm whale, whose vestigial "fingers" are visible in its flippers. Nearby, a mock-up of a small nineteenth-century whaleboat is fully labeled with its various esoteric components and gadgets. Both serve by way of introduction to the gripping, if somewhat grisly, Whale Museum, which takes up half the mall's uppermost floor (daily 9am–10pm; free).

This free exhibition is devoted to Maui's former heyday as a whaling center, illustrating the tedium and the terror of the seamen's daily routine through scrimshaw, shellwork valentines, logbooks, tools, letters, and bills. As well as a scale model of the whaling bark *Sunbeam*, there's a large cast-iron "try pot"; though used for reducing whale blubber at sea, they gave rise to the stereotyped but not entirely untrue image of cannibals cooking missionaries in big black cauldrons. Contrary to what you might imagine, no actual killing of whales took place in Hawaiian waters. Hawaii was simply the place where the whaling ships came to recuperate after hunting much further north in the Pacific. What's more, the humpback – the whale most commonly found in Hawaiian waters – was not hunted at all during the nineteenth century. The target for the fleets was instead the right whale, so named, logically enough, because it was deemed the "right" whale to kill.

▲ WHALE MUSEUM

Shops

Whalers Village

While even the most inveterate shopper would probably not bother to drive to Kāʻanapali just to visit the Whalers Village mall, it does hold a reasonable array of stores, almost all geared towards tourists. Martin & MacArthur is good for Hawaiian crafts and tiki-style souvenirs; there's a Borders Express with several shelves of Hawaii-related books and maps; Lahaina Printsellers stock good maps and prints; Reyn's has well-priced aloha wear; and you'll also find international chains like the Body Shop and Louis Vuitton. Besides the restaurants reviewed below, there's a food court on the lower level with Korean, Japanese, and Italian outlets, plus an espresso bar and a *McDonald's*.

Restaurants

Hula Grill

Whalers Village ☎808/667-6636. Daily 11am–9.30pm. This large oceanfront restaurant, open to the sea breezes and offering great views at lunchtime, features live Hawaiian music nightly. Chef Peter Merriman, who is known for his distinctively Hawaiian take on things, prepares some interesting appetizers, such as a Hawaiian ceviche, marinated in lime, Maui onion, and coconut milk ($8), along with plenty of dim sum and sashimi, while the $18–34 entrees include a $27 coconut seafood chowder.

Rusty Harpoon

Whalers Village ☎808/661-3123. Daily 8am–10pm. A mall restaurant, set slightly back from the sea but enjoying good views from both terrace and covered seating. The lunch menu combines inexpensive standards like burgers and sandwiches with inventive specials, such as a seafood curry casserole ($20); traditional dinner entrees of steaks, ribs, and fresh fish cost $23–33. A $17 set dinner menu is served 5–6pm only.

Son'z Maui at Swan Court

Hyatt Regency Maui, 200 Nohea Kai Drive ☎808/667-4506. Sun–Thurs 5–10pm, Fri & Sat 5–10.30pm. The *Hyatt's* sublimely romantic *Swan Court* restaurant, laid out around a lagoon populated by live swans and flamingoes, has been revamped under this clumsy name to signal its desire to serve "classic cuisine for the next generation". The food

PLACES Kāʻanapali

▼ SON'Z MAUI AT SWAN COURT

PLACES

Kā'anapali

▲ DRUMS OF THE PACIFIC

is as good as ever, but now the menu is part Pacific Rim, with appetizers like tiger-eye sushi ($17) and New Zealand mussels ($14), and some great fish entrees at $32–40, and part Mediterranean, with standards like *coq au vin* ($32) or grilled steak for two ($79).

Tiki Terrace

Kā'anapali Beach Hotel, 2525 Kā'anapali Parkway ☎808/667-0124. Daily 7–10am & 5–9.30pm. This unassuming hotel restaurant attempts to serve traditional Hawaiian foods, meaning plenty of fish, plus local ingredients like *taro* and sweet potato, and much of it steamed in *ti*-leaf parcels. Although that sounds like a good idea, and the food itself isn't bad, the open-air "tiki grill" section makes it a favorite with families with young kids, and as a result it tends to be both hectic and messy. In the evening, when there's somewhat cheesy Hawaiian entertainment, the set Hawaiian dinner menu

costs $23, or you can order Westernized entrees like BBQ ribs or New York steak for $19–45.

Shows

Drums of the Pacific

Hyatt Regency Maui, Kā'anapali ☎808/661-1234. Daily 5pm, adults $89, teenagers $58, under-13s $45. If you're looking for the full *lū'au* experience, you won't get it from the *Hyatt Regency*'s evening show. Though it's set just yards from the sea, guests remain seated at long tables throughout, so you barely even see the sunset. The buffet-style food is pretty good, but the menu is very limited and there's barely an attempt to explain its Hawaiian origins or traditions. The show itself, however, isn't bad, with a full panoply of hula dancers and Polynesian performers, climaxing in a display of fire-eating.

Northwest Maui

Heavily developed in stretches with mostly smaller-scale condos and homes, the coastline of Northwest Maui is home to idyllic beaches – though they're not often easily spotted through all the resorts. Even within a few miles of Kā'anapali the rainfall becomes significantly heavier. While the landscape grows greener, development peters out altogether beyond upscale Kapalua. The road continues to the legendary surf spot of Honolua Bay, before dwindling to a single lane as the Kahekili Highway. On the map, this looks like a good route to Wailuku, but it's a dangerous drive and far from a shortcut; you have to allow well over an hour for the journey. That said, while not quite matching the road to Hāna (see p.126), the Kahekili Highway is exhilaratingly beautiful, providing a rare glimpse of how Maui must have looked before the advent of tourism.

Honokōwai, Kahana, and Nāpili

The three communities of Honokōwai, Kahana, and Nāpili that appear on maps just north of Kā'anapali are only nominally distinct; each blends seamlessly into the next, and none holds an ounce of interest for casual visitors. Ignored by the main highway as it heads for Kapalua and beyond, they're linked by Lower Honoapi'ilani Road, which branches down towards the ocean about a mile out of Kā'anapali. To its left stands a succession of all but identical hotels, to its right you'll find the occasional little mall holding one or two stores or restaurants.

Nāpili Bay

This half-mile crescent of perfect if steeply shelving white sand, commanding beautiful views across to Molokai, is filled each day with families staying at adjacent hotels like the *Mauian*. The waves that break right on shore can be pretty fierce, and

▼ NĀPILI BAY

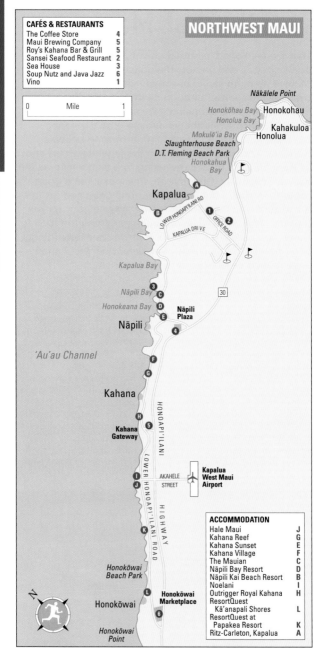

CAFÉS & RESTAURANTS

The Coffee Store	4
Maui Brewing Company	5
Roy's Kahana Bar & Grill	5
Sansei Seafood Restaurant	2
Sea House	3
Soup Nutz and Java Jazz	6
Vino	1

NORTHWEST MAUI

0   Mile   1

Nākālele Point

Honokōhau Bay   Honokohau
Honolua Bay
Kahakuloa
Mokulē'ia Bay   Honolua
Slaughterhouse Beach
D.T. Fleming Beach Park
Honokahua
Bay

Kapalua

LOWER HONOAPI'ILANI RD
KAPALUA DRIVE   OFFICE ROAD

Kapalua Bay

Nāpili Bay
Honokeana Bay   Nāpili
Plaza

Nāpili

'Au'au Channel

Kahana

HONOAPI'ILANI

Kahana
Gateway

LOWER HONOAPI'ILANI HIGHWAY

AKAHELE
STREET   Kapalua
West Maui
Airport

Honokōwai
Beach Park

Honokōwai   Honokōwai
Marketplace

Honokōwai
Point

N

ACCOMMODATION

Hale Maui	J
Kahana Reef	G
Kahana Sunset	E
Kahana Village	F
The Mauian	C
Nāpili Bay Resort	D
Nāpili Kai Beach Resort	B
Noelani	I
Outrigger Royal Kahana	H
ResortQuest at Kā'anapali Shores	L
ResortQuest at Papakea Resort	K
Ritz-Carleton, Kapalua	A

there's often a strong undertow too, but the snorkeling a little further out is excellent, especially in the morning, and there's plenty of shelter from both wind and sun.

Kapalua Beach

Kapalua, at the end of Lower Honoapi'ilani Road in Maui's far northwest corner, is the West Maui equivalent of the exclusive resort of Wailea, at the southwest tip of East Maui. Relatively few tourists stray into this pristine enclave, whose luxurious hotels capitalize well on their proximity to Kapalua Beach. A perfect little arc of white sand, set between two rocky headlands, it is frequently voted the best beach in the US. Besides being pretty, it's also one of Maui's safest beaches, especially good for snorkeling and diving, and even receives occasional visits from monk seals. The one drawback to Kapalua is that the climate is undeniably worse even this short distance north of Lahaina, with rain and cloud more likely to drift in from the northeast.

D.T. Fleming Beach Park

Honoapi'ilani Highway sweeps down beyond Kapalua to rejoin the ocean at D.T. Fleming Beach Park, in Honokahua Bay. The dunes here, knitted together with ironwood trees, drop sharply into the sea, and swimming can be dangerous – though surfers love the big waves. Full park amenities, including showers, restrooms, picnic tables, and the presence of lifeguards, make this a popular destination for local families.

Slaughterhouse Beach

Beyond Honokahua Bay, the highway climbs again to cross

a rocky headland. You can't see it from the road, but Mokulē'ia Bay lies at the foot of the cliffs. At several points along the highway, the landowners, Maui Pineapple, have built fences to stop people from clambering down through the undergrowth to shaded, sandy Slaughterhouse Beach. Keep your eyes peeled instead for the top of the concrete stairway that provides safe access; look for cars parked on the verge. Winter conditions usually preclude bathing, but nude sunbathing carries on year-round.

Honolua Bay

Both Mokulē'ia Bay and Honolua Bay, just past the point, have been set aside as a Marine Life Conservation District, and in summer offer some of the island's best snorkeling. Honolua's major claim to fame, however, is as Maui's most heralded surfing spot, and between September

▲ D.T. FLEMING BEACH PARK

and April, the waters regularly swarm with surfers. As long as the swell remains below five feet, intermediate surfers can enjoy some of the longest-lasting and most predictable waves in all Hawaii. When they exceed ten feet, however, only absolute experts can hope to survive; perils include not only a fearsome cave that seems to suck in every passing stray, but cut-throat competition from other surfers. Parking for surfers is at several ad hoc lots along the graded dirt roads that line the fields covering the headland on the far side of the bay. Large galleries of spectators assemble on the clifftop to watch the action, while the surfers themselves slither down to the ocean by means of treacherous trails.

To reach the beach at Honolua, park instead beside the road at the inland end of the bay and walk down. The access path is the width of a road, but the surface is terrible and driving on it is illegal. Taking it will lead you through a weird, lush forest with the feel of a Louisiana bayou; every tree, and even the barbed-wire fence, has been throttled by creeping vines. Across a (usually dry) streambed lies the neat, rocky curve of the beach itself, consisting largely of dark black rocks, with the eastern end of Molokai framed in the mouth of the bay. The snorkelers who congregate at Honolua whenever the waves die down generally ease themselves in from the beach, but then have to swim a fair way out beyond the clear turquoise inshore waters to reach the coves and coral on the left side of the bay.

Honokōhau Bay

Beyond here Honoapi'ilani Highway runs past one final beach, at Honokōhau Bay. You're still only five miles out of Kapalua here, but it feels like another world. The entire valley is swamped by a dense canopy of flowering trees; there's a hidden village in there, but it's hard to spot a single building. The beach itself is a small crescent of gray pebbles, used only by fishermen.

Nākālele Point

Just over a mile past Honokōhau Bay and 6.5 miles out of Kapalua, at milepost 38, the Kahekili Highway begins at Maui's northernmost limit, Nākālele Point. This rolling expanse of grassy heathland fell

▼ NĀKĀLELE POINT

victim several years ago to a bizarre craze that swept most of Hawaii. In remote spots all over the islands, people suddenly started erecting miniature stone cairns, under the impression that they were maintaining an ancient tradition. Stacks of perhaps a dozen small rocks are dotted all over the landscape, and many visitors have also used pebbles to spell out their names or other messages – much to the displeasure of Maui Pineapple, which still owns the land.

Various deeply rutted dirt roads drop away from the highway towards the sea in this area, starting both from the parking lot at milepost 38 and from another more makeshift lot half a mile further on. Hiking in that direction enables you to inspect the small light beacon that warns passing ships of the rocky headland, and an impressive natural blowhole in the oceanfront shelf. Be very, very wary of approaching the water, however; several hikers have been swept off the rocks by rogue waves in recent years.

Kahakuloa

Beyond Nākālele Point, the Kahekili Highway seems to wind endlessly along the extravagantly indented coastline. Often very narrow, but always smoothly surfaced, it alternates between scrubby exposed promontories, occasionally capable of supporting a pale meadow, and densely green, wet valleys.

A few miles along, the huge and very un-Hawaiian-looking crag of Kahakuloa Head towers 636ft above the eastern entrance to Kahakuloa Bay. The name means "tall lord," on account of its supposed resemblance to a member of the chiefly class, the *ali'i*, wearing a feathered cape; alongside it stands his attendant, a lesser peak known as Pu'u Kāhuli'anapa. The verdant valley that stretches back from both once ranked among the most populous on Maui, and still looks like a classic *ahupua'a* – the fundamental ancient land division, reaching from the sea to the mountain via low-lying taro terraces and groves of palms and fruit trees.

The perfect little village of Kahakuloa is poised just behind its beach of black and gray boulders. Close to the green clapboard church as you drive in, a couple of fruit stands, laden with fresh pineapples and other goodies, make tempting places to stop. The streambed is lined with trees, while dirt roads crisscross the valley between the fields and the ramshackle houses. A little further back nestles the simple wooden structures of St Francis Xavier Mission, built in 1846.

Cafés

The Coffee Store

Nāpili Plaza, 5095 Nāpili Hau St, Nāpili ☎808/669-4170, ⓦwww .mauicoffee.com. Daily 6.30am–11pm. Small espresso bar, busy with active locals from 6.30am daily, which as well as pastries and sandwiches also offers Internet access.

Restaurants

Maui Brewing Company

Kahana Gateway, 4405 Honoapi'ilani Hwy ☎808/669-3474. Daily 11am–1am. Large mall complex consisting of a pub serving pilsners, stouts, and wheat beers brewed on the premises, and an open restaurant area dominated by a *kiawe* grill

▲ SEA HOUSE

and an oyster bar. The food is surprisingly good for mall fare, with grilled ribs or chicken for under $20, a one-pound prime rib for $28, and fresh fish prepared in various styles for around $28. A lighter, limited menu is served during the afternoon and until 1am nightly.

Roy's Kahana Bar & Grill

Kahana Gateway, 4405 Honoapi'ilani Hwy ☎ 808/669-6999, ⊛ www .roysrestaurant.com. Daily 5.30–10pm. Celebrity chef Roy Yamaguchi's Maui showcase is open for dinner only – which is just as well, given its lack of views. The aromas of its superb "Euro-Asian" food waft from its open kitchen as soon as you walk in. Signature dishes such as hibachi salmon, "butterfish" (black cod) steamed with *miso*, and "Roy's 'Original' Blackened Rare *Ahi*" appear on the menu as both appetizers (around $12) and entrees ($25–30); there are also several mouthwatering specials each night.

Sansei Seafood Restaurant

600 Office Rd, Kapalua ☎ 808/669-6286. Mon–Wed, Sat & Sun 5.30–10pm, Thurs & Fri 5.30pm–1am. Top-quality, dinner-only seafood and sushi specialist, which also has

an outlet in Kīhei (see p.96). Ensconced in spacious new premises, *Sansei* is fundamentally Japanese, though there's a strong Pacific Rim element as well. The fresh sushi selection includes a mouthwatering mango crab salad roll ($8), while a delicious prawn and scallops pasta ($20), and daily fish specials ($25) are among the entrees. There's also karaoke until 1am on Thursday and Friday nights.

Sea House

Nāpili Kai Beach Resort, 5500 Lower Honoapi'ilani Rd, Nāpili ☎ 808/669-1500. Mon & Wed–Sun 8–10.30am, 11.30am– 2pm, & 6–9pm; Tues 5.30–9pm. Very popular seafront restaurant, right on Nāpili Beach at the most upscale of the oceanside hotels. The food is good without being exceptional – conventional American breakfasts for around $10; lunchtime soups, salads, sandwiches, or sushi rolls for $9–14; and steak or seafood dinner entrees costing anything from $23 to $40 – but the views, from the oceanside tables at least, and especially at sunset, are totally fabulous. Every Tuesday at 5.30pm, local kids put on a display of *hula* and Hawaiian culture, in a separate marquee, for $10.

Soup Nutz and Java Jazz

Honokōwai Marketplace, 3350 Lower Honoapiʻilani Rd ☎ 808/667-0787, Ⓦ www.javajazz.net. Mon–Sat 6am–9pm, Sun 6am–5pm. At first glance, you'd think this funky mall hangout is just a juice and espresso bar, but it actually serves pretty good food throughout the day, and with lots of comfy seating and a steady jazz soundtrack you may well feel tempted to linger despite the lack of views. The menu includes breakfast eggs and omelets ($8–12); smoothies ($5); falafel and other lunchtime sandwiches (under $10); and evening specials that range up to steak and lobster ($22–33).

Vino

Kapalua Village Golf Course Clubhouse, Office Rd, Kapalua ☎ 808/661-8466. Daily 5.30–9.30pm. Though this surprising but superb restaurant, just off the main highway above the Ritz-Carlton resorts, is the brainchild of the Japanese chef/owner of the nearby *Sansei* (see opposite), here the specialty is Italian, not sushi. Or rather, Italian with a definite Hawaiian tinge, with ingredients like Kona lobster and raw *ahi* alongside the pasta and gnocchi dishes. Two further characteristics distinguish the menu: a large selection of *tapas*-sized portions, most costing $7–10, which enable you to sample several very disparate dishes, and the particular attention afforded to wine, with special pairings devised for most dishes. If you prefer a more conventional meal, a "large plate" – a full-sized entree, such as osso bucco or horseradish-crusted short rib – costs $19–25. A "Taste of *Vino*" menu offers the pick of the best for two people for $65, though it's not cheaper than ordering *à la carte.*

The one drawback is that its golf-course clubhouse setting lacks atmosphere.

Shows

Masters of Hawaiian Slack Key Guitar

Nāpili Kai Beach Resort, 5900 Lower Honoapiʻilani Rd, Naāpili ☎ 808/669-3858 or 1-888/669-3858, Ⓦ www .slackkey.com. Wed 7.30pm, $45, Hawaii residents $35. This ongoing series of slack-key guitar concerts is an absolute treat. Presenting traditional Hawaiian music in a gorgeous oceanfront setting, the evenings are gloriously happy events, thanks in large part to virtuoso MC George Kahumoku, Jr. Each week sees a different guest star, from the very biggest names of the genre – regulars include Cyril Pahinui, Led Kaʻapana, and Dennis Kamakahi – and live recordings of the concerts have three times won Grammies. It's possible that during the lifetime of this book, the concerts will return to their former home, the nearby *Ritz-Carlton* in Kapalua; call ahead to check the current location.

▲ MASTERS OF HAWAIIAN SLACK KEY GUITAR

Kahului

Although Kahului is the largest town on Maui – it holds the island's principal harbor and airport, and most of its major shopping centers – it's not an interesting, let alone historic, place to visit. A couple of inexpensive hotels stake a claim for Kahului as a central base, but there's little to see here, and you could miss it altogether with a clear conscience. That said, you'll probably find yourself calling in repeatedly, to buy supplies, grab a snack as you race round the island, or perhaps attend a show at the prestigious Maui Arts and Cultural Center. Locals are waiting to see whether the daily ferry services from Oahu will revitalize the town's economy.

Maui Arts and Cultural Center

1 Cameron Way, Kahului Beach Rd, Kahului ☏ 808/242-2787, box office ☏ 808/242-7469, ⓦ www.mauiarts.org.

Just off the busy Kahului Beach Road, which curves around Kahului Harbor, the Maui Arts and Cultural Center is Maui's

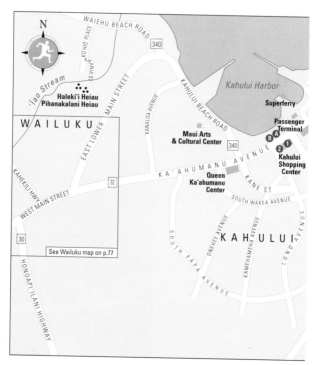

Maui's main port

Having started the nineteenth century as a small cluster of grass shacks, Kahului grew in tandem with the expansion of commercial agriculture. After the Kahului and Wailuku Railroad opened in 1879, it channeled the sugar and pineapple crops of central Maui down to the wharves of Kahului. At first Kahului was an unsanitary place: a major outbreak of plague in 1900 forced the authorities to burn down the oceanfront Chinatown district and ring the whole town with rat-proof fences. When it was rebuilt, the harbor was greatly expanded and dredged to provide the only deep-water anchorage on the island.

Kahului thereafter supplanted Lahaina as Maui's main port and has remained so to this day, welcoming both an ever-increasing number of cruise ship passengers as well as the Superferry services detailed on p.170. Kahului was further boosted after World War II, when newly built, low-cost housing in "Dream City" lured laborers away from plantation towns such as Pā'ia with the promise that they would have their own homes.

premier venue for the visual and performing arts. In addition to a four-thousand-seat open-air amphitheater, it houses two separate indoor theaters and an art gallery that hosts changing temporary exhibitions. Those big-name musicians who make it as far as Maui – more than you might expect, as it's a favorite

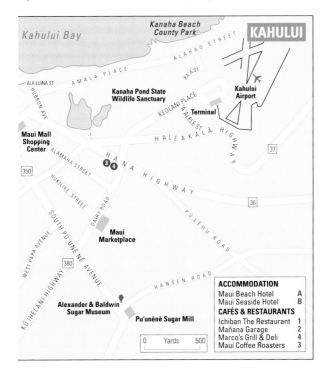

final stop for trans-America touring bands – play here, while the Maui Symphony Orchestra (☏808/244-5439) puts on half a dozen concerts each winter.

In addition, the center's Castle Theater operates as a movie theater in conjunction with the Maui Film Festival (☏808/572-3456, ⓦwww.mauifilmfestival.com). The festival itself takes place in Wailea each June, but every Wednesday evening the Castle Theater shows a current release, and each December it also puts on nightly "Academy Screenings" of potential Oscar contenders.

Kanahā Pond State Wildlife Sanctuary

Half a mile west of Kahului Airport, just before Hwy-36A meets Hwy-36, a tiny roadside parking lot marks the only public access to the Kanahā Pond State Wildlife Sanctuary. This marshy saltwater lagoon – used as a fishpond until it was choked by the mud dredged up from Kahului Harbor – is now set aside for the protection of endangered bird species, among them the black-necked *aeʻo* stilt and the *ʻaukuʻu* (night heron).

There are no official opening hours; visitors simply make their way through the gate and follow a pedestrian causeway for fifty yards out to a windy, open-sided viewing shelter. Although it's not a very prepossessing spot, with the factories of Kahului Harbor clearly visible off to the left, and planes passing low overhead as they descend into the airport, it's surprisingly peaceful, and waterfowl do indeed seem to like it. Wading birds can almost always be spotted picking their way through the shallow waters, though when it comes to smaller species you're likely to hear more than you actually see.

Kanahā Beach County Park

Due east of central Kahului, Amala Place runs through an industrial area behind Kanahā Pond. Even on the ocean side of the airport, before the road joins Alahao Street, you'll find plenty of places where you can park beside the road and walk through the trees to find a long strip of empty beach.

However, the most popular oceanfront spot is the large Kanahā Beach County Park which, despite its proximity to the runways, is completely undisturbed by all the comings and goings and feels comfortably far from Kahului. Its shallow, choppy turquoise waters are ideal for novice windsurfers, who come from all over the world to swirl back and forth against the backdrop of ʻĪao Valley and the West Maui mountains. Among companies offering windsurfing lessons here (at around $80 for 2hr 30min, including equipment rental) are Action Sports Maui

▼ KANAHĀ BEACH COUNTY PARK

(☎808/871-5857, ⓦwww
.actionsportsmaui.com), and Alan
Cadiz's HST Windsurfing School
(☎808/871-5423 or 1-800/968-
5423, ⓦwww.hstwindsurfing
.com). Windsurfers ready for the
big time graduate to Ho'okipa,
just a few miles east but light-
years away in terms of difficulty;
see p.126.

For its full, considerable length,
the beach is fringed by pine
trees, with countless shoots
sprouting from the dunes and
fallen needles creating a soft
carpet just behind. Local clubs
keep their outrigger canoes here,
and you're likely to see them
practicing. The lawns under the
trees have picnic tables, though
to buy food or drink you have to
drive back into Kahului. There is
also a campground, administered
by the county parks office (see
p.166), with seven individual
sites ($3 per night) limited to
a three-night maximum stay.
However, the combination of
being right next to the airport,
and also its potential exposure to
crime, thanks to the proximity
to Kahului, makes it hard to
recommend.

Alexander & Baldwin Sugar Museum

3957 Hansen Rd, Pu'unēnē
☎808/871-8058, ⓦwww
.sugarmuseum.com. Mon–Sat 9.30am–
4.30pm; $5, under-18s $2. There's
no missing the rusty red hulk of
the Pu'unēnē Sugar Mill, which
forces Hwy-350 to make a
sharp right turn a mile south of
Kahului. Still belching smoke as
it consumes the cane from the
surrounding fields, this was the
largest sugar mill in the world
when it was built in 1902, and
now stands as one of only two
such mills still operational in
Hawaii – the other is on Kauai.
Easily overlooked, however, is

the smaller building just across
from the mill, at the intersection
with the minor Hansen Road,
which houses the Alexander &
Baldwin Sugar Museum.

The museum relates the history
of sugar production on Maui,
a tale of nineteenth-century
scheming and skulduggery that,
well over a century later, may
not be capable of holding your
interest for very long. Scale
models include a whirring but
incomprehensible re-creation of
the main mill machinery, and a
relief map of the whole island.
More illuminating displays focus
on the lives of the plantation
laborers, showing the thick
clothes they wore to protect
against the dust and poisonous
centipedes, and the numbered
bango tags by which they were
identified in place of names.
No bones are made of the fact
that the multi-ethnic workforce
was deliberately, but ultimately
unsuccessfully, segregated to avoid
solidarity. The museum store
is well stocked with books on
ethnic and labor history, as well as
souvenir packets of raw sugar.

Shops

Maui Marketplace

Away from central Kahului,
the Maui Marketplace mall on
Dairy Road is noteworthy as
the home of the island's best
bookstore – a giant Borders
(Mon–Thurs 9am–11pm, Fri
& Sat 9am–midnight, Sun
9am–10pm; ☎808/877-6160).

Queen Ka'ahumanu Center

275 Ka'ahumanu Ave, Kahului
☎808/877-3369, ⓦwww
.queenkaahumanucenter.com.
Kahului's smartest and largest
shopping mall, the Queen
Ka'ahumanu Center, is located

▲ QUEEN KAʻAHUMANU CENTER

just across from the harbor. Anchored by Macy's and Sears department stores, it also holds a fair assortment of specialty stores, including the surf and beach wear of Local Motion and a Borders Express. Various upscale restaurants and bars have tried to establish themselves here only to falter within a year or two, but there is a reasonable open-air food court upstairs.

Cafés

Maui Coffee Roasters

444 Hāna Hwy ☎808/877-2877. Mon–Fri 7am–6pm, Sat 8am–5pm, Sun 8am–2.30pm. This relaxed, daytime-only espresso bar with hand-painted tables is a popular hangout for windsurfers from the nearby beaches. Vegetarian wraps and sandwiches, like focaccia with mozzarella, are $6–8; try the fabulous raspberry-and-white-chocolate scones.

▼ MAUI COFFEE ROASTERS

Restaurants

Ichiban The Restaurant

Kahului Shopping Center, 47 Kaʻahumanu Ave ☎808/871-6977. Mon–Fri 7am–2pm & 5–9pm, Sat 10.30am–2pm & 5–9pm. Large mall eatery, which serves American and continental breakfasts, then devotes itself for the remainder of the day to Japanese cuisine. For lunch there's *saimin* for $6, *donburi* bowls for $7, and teriyakis for $6–9; at dinner you can get shrimp or chicken stir-fries, *udon* noodles, and sushi rolls for under $10.

Mañana Garage

33 Lono Ave ☎808/873-0220. Mon 11am–9pm, Tues–Fri 11am–10.30pm, Sat 5–10.30pm, Sun 5–9pm. This Latin American–Mexican restaurant, kitted out with a cheery, vaguely post-industrial decor and located in an office building right on Kaʻahumanu Avenue, serves a creative but somewhat overpriced menu ranging from fish tacos to guava salmon to paella. It's popular with locals for lunch, and, thanks to a spacious (albeit viewless) terrace, for after-work drinks. Typical entrees cost around $12 for lunch, up to $30 in the evening. Live music and dancing most nights.

Marco's Grill & Deli

395 Dairy Rd ☎808/877-4446. Daily 7.30am–10pm. Lively Italian restaurant, in a modern mall not far from the airport. Once the breakfast omelets, pancakes, and espressos have finished, the lunch and dinner menus feature deli sandwiches, pizzas (from $12), and rich meat and seafood pastas, including rigatoni with prosciutto in a vodka sauce ($19).

Wailuku

Located at the mouth of the fertile and spectacular 'Īao Valley and within a few miles of the lush valleys that line the windward coast of West Maui, Wailuku has a very different geography to, and a much more venerable history than, its close neighbor to the east, Kahului. This was what might be called the *poi* bowl of Maui, at the heart of the largest *taro*-growing area in Hawaii, and was home to generations of priests and warriors in ancient times. These days Wailuku is a sleepy sort of place, easily seen in less than half a day. Nonetheless, it's one of the few towns on Maui that still feels like a genuine community, and can serve as a welcome antidote to the sanitized charms of the modern resorts elsewhere.

Downtown Wailuku

The heart of Wailuku is where Main Street, the continuation of Ka'ahumanu Avenue, crosses Market Street. Both streets hold a small assortment of shops, the most interesting of which are the faded antique and junk stores along Market Street to the north, just before it drops down to cross the 'Īao Stream. Also look for the 1929 'Īao Theater,

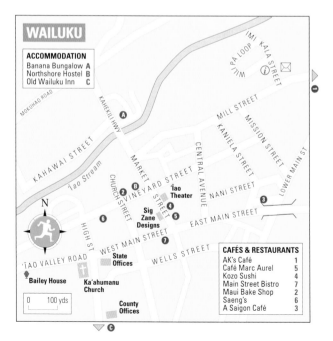

▲ DOWNTOWN WAILUKU

an attractive little playhouse on Market Street that typically puts on six Broadway-type shows each year (season runs Sept–June; ☏808/242-6969, Ⓦwww .mauionstage.com).

Ka'ahumanu Church, at the intersection of Main and High streets just west of the center, was founded in 1832. Naming it after Queen Ka'ahumanu, a convert to Christianity who was largely responsible for the destruction of the old Hawaiian religion (see p.137), was the idea of the Queen herself. The current building, whose four-story white spire has a clock face on each side, dates from 1876. It's not usually open to visitors, but you're welcome to attend the Hawaiian-language services at 9am on Sunday mornings.

The Bailey House

2375-A Main St ☏808/244-3326, Ⓦwww.mauimuseum.org. Mon–Sat 10am–4pm; $5, ages 7–13 $1, under-7s free. The Bailey House, to the left on Main Street as it starts to climb west out of Wailuku as 'Iao Valley Road, is the best museum of general history on Maui. The oldest house on the island, it sits on what was once Maui's most highly prized plot

of land. A royal compound here formerly controlled access to the sacred 'Iao Valley. Local chiefs donated it during the 1830s so the Central Maui Mission could build day schools to teach both adults and children to read. From 1837 until 1849, it was also the site of the Wailuku Female Seminary, a boarding school designed to produce "good Christian wives" for the male graduates of the Lahainaluna Seminary (see p.53).

The first occupant of the house was Reverend Jonathan Green, who resigned from the mission in 1842 to protest the fact that the American Board of Commissioners for Foreign Missions accepted money from slave-owners. For the next fifty years, it was home to Edward Bailey and his wife Caroline Hubbard Bailey. He was a minister, schoolmaster, carpenter, and amateur painter, while she is remembered in the name of the long "Mother Hubbard" dresses, also known as *mu'umu'us*, that she made for local women.

After an entertaining introductory talk, visitors can wander through rooms filled with period furniture, none of which originally belonged here. The largest room focuses on ancient Hawaiian history, with archeological finds from Maui, Lanai, and Kahoolawe, including bones, clubs, shark's-tooth weapons, and *leis* of shells and feathers. One large wooden platter was used for serving boiled dog – a popular dish for native Hawaiian women, who were forbidden to eat pork. There's also a copy of the only carved temple image ever found on Maui, a likeness of the pig-god Kamapua'a that was discovered in a remote Upcountry cave. Both the Baileys and the ancient Hawaiians alike would be appalled to see such a sacred item on public display. On the wall there's a portrait of the unruly chief Boki, who sailed to the South Seas in 1829 in search of sandalwood to replace Hawaii's vanished crop and died in an explosion at sea.

A gallery downstairs holds local landscapes painted by the white-bearded Edward Bailey in his old age, while the upstairs rooms are preserved more or less as the Baileys would have known them, with a quilt of the Hawaiian flag spread across the four-poster bed. Presumably, however, they'd disavow the opium pipe and paraphernalia displayed at one point.

Haleki'i and Pihanakalani heiaus

Hea Place; daily 7am–7pm; free.

A mile from central Wailuku – but over three miles by road – the twin ancient temples of Haleki'i and Pihanakalani guard the Wailuku Plain from two separate hillocks near the mouth of the 'Iao Stream. They can only be reached via a very convoluted route; follow Hwy-333 all the way out of Wailuku to the north, double back south

along Waiehu Beach Road, turn inland at Kuhio Place, and take the first left, Hea Place.

With rows of low-budget housing to the north, and the industrial area of Kahului to the south, this is not the most evocative of sites, but raising your gaze towards the horizon provides fine views of the ocean and the turquoise waters of the harbor and, in the early morning, mighty Haleakalā can often be seen in its entirety. The short trail from the parking lot leads through scrubby soil – these hillocks are, in fact, lithified sand dunes – to Haleki'i Heiau. Maui's ruling chief, Kahekili, lived at this "house of images" during religious ceremonies in the 1760s, when its uppermost platform would have held thatched huts interspersed with carved effigies of the gods. The hilltop is now bare, and the only remnants of the *heiau* are the lower stone terraces dropping down the side towards Kahului.

Both Haleki'i and Pihanakalani *heiaus* were *luakinis*, or temples dedicated to the war god Ku that were the site of human sacrifices. Pihanakalani seems to have been

▼ THE BAILEY HOUSE

originally constructed sometime between 1260 and 1400 AD, and reoriented to face towards the Big Island during the eighteenth century, which archeologists see as a sign that the chiefs of Maui must have been preparing an attack. When Kamehameha the Great's Big Island warriors finally conquered Maui in 1790, they celebrated their victory at 'Iao Valley (see p.85) with a rededication ceremony at Pihanakalani that included its final human sacrifice. Like all ancient Hawaiian temples, it was stripped of its images and largely dismantled after the death of Kamehameha, which coincided with the arrival of the first Christian missionaries. Significantly more traces survive than of Haleki'i, however, so it's worth continuing this far, by following the main path to the far side of the gulch and then turning left.

Waihe'e Valley Trail

At times during the past few years, it has been possible to drive half a mile inland from Waihe'e on Waihe'e Valley Road, and then take a two-hour hike up into the rainforest of Waihe'e Valley itself. When this book went to press, however, the major local landowner, Wailuku Agriculture, had chosen to deny all access to the area. The trail is one of Maui's finest, so it might be worth calling them on ☎808/244-9570, or simply driving in, to see whether they've decided to start allowing visitors once again. If so, you can expect to pay a trail fee of around $5, and only consider coming on fine days; if rain is at all likely, there's a serious risk of flash floods on portions of the trail.

Waihe'e Ridge Trail

One of Maui's most enjoyable hikes, the Waihe'e Ridge Trail, starts a mile up a spur road that branches *mauka* (inland) from Kahekili Highway at mile post 7, opposite the Mendes Ranch three miles north of the village school in Waihe'e. If you get here by driving the Kahekili Highway around West Maui from Kapalua – see p.65 – you'll find the turning, which is signposted to *Camp Maluhia*, roughly seven miles south of Kahakuloa.

This gorgeous climb, best done in the morning before the clouds set in, takes you as high into the West Maui mountains as it's possible to go; allow at least two hours, and preferably three, for the round trip. From the easily spotted parking lot where the road makes a sharp curve right towards the camp itself, the trail starts off as a very clear cement path beyond a barred gate. This is its steepest section, but it soon comes to an end, when you turn left to find yourself in a pine and eucalyptus forest. Before long you emerge from that in turn, to enjoy views down into Waihe'e Valley, over to a double waterfall embedded

▼ WAIHE'E VALLEY TRAIL

▲ WAIHE'E RIDGE TRAIL

in the next ridge to the north, and back across the isthmus to Haleakalā Highway snaking up the volcano.

For all this first stretch of the trail, which totals 1.5 miles, it looks as though you're heading for the crest of the ridge ahead. Ultimately, however, the path sidesteps across a brief razorback to reach an unexpected high mountain valley. The terrain here is extremely marshy, but you're soon climbing again, this time through tree-less uplands that feature a much more greater preponderance of native Hawaiian plants and shrubs, including some spectacular orchids and also stunted red- and orange-blossomed *lehua* trees.

The trail ends at an unsheltered picnic table in a clearing 2.25 miles up. The chances are that by now you're well above the cloud line. If you're lucky enough to be here on a clear morning, however, you can see most of northern Maui from this spot, which is the summit of Lanilili ("Small Heaven") Peak but still well short of the overall summit of West Maui. Towering cliffs and waterfalls lie ahead, while as you look north towards the ocean the island of Molokai is clearly visible beyond the rocky pinnacle of Kahakuloa.

Shops

Sig Zane Designs

53 Market St ☎808/249-8997, ⓦwww.sigzane.com. Sig Zane is a Big Island textile designer renowned for the elegant simplicity of his fabrics, each of which is strongly rooted in the lore of native Hawaiian plants. As well as the classiest aloha wear to be found in Hawaii, his shop also sells bedding, slippers, and other household goods.

Cafés

Café Marc Aurel

28 N Market St ☎808/244-0852. Mon–Sat 7am–9pm. Smart and very popular sidewalk café,

▼ SIG ZANE DESIGNS

serving espressos, smoothies, and pastries, and also offering Internet access.

Maui Bake Shop & Deli

2092 Vineyard St ☎ 808/244-7117. Tues–Fri 6.30am–2.30pm, Sat 7am–1pm. French-style *patisserie* serving healthy deli breakfasts and lunches, with a wide assortment of soups, salads, and quiches, as well as wonderful fresh-baked breads, including focaccias, calzones, whole-grain loaves, and sweet brioches. You can eat well for $5 or less.

Restaurants

AK's Cafe

1237 L Market St ☎ 808/244-8774, ☻ www.akscafe.com. Tues–Fri 11am–2.30pm & 5–9pm, Sat 5–9pm. This bright, clean and highly recommended little restaurant, well away from downtown on the road up from Kahului Harbor, has a mission to improve the health of local residents, with an emphasis on steaming or grilling rather than frying. Great-value lunch specials at $7–9, such as the succulent baked *ono*, and $12–18 dinner entrees like crab cakes, seared *ahi* or lemongrass duck breast, come with two sides, such as *taro* or *ulu* (breadfruit).

Kozo Sushi

52 N Market St ☎ 808/243-5696. Mon–Sat 10am–6pm. Clean, attractive central sushi place that mainly provides takeout for local office workers, but also has a couple of tables where you can enjoy tasty and very well priced individual rolls ($2 or less), a *nigiri* lunch box ($6.50), or Hawaii's very own spam *musubi* – spam, seaweed, and rice ($1.30).

Main Street Bistro

2051 Main St ☎ 808/244-6816. Mon–Fri 11am–3pm. The chef/ owner of this simple, roomy lunch-only café on Wailuku's somewhat neglected Main Street has an impressive record with Maui's top restaurants, and now prepares good-value, healthy but filling meals for appreciative locals. Salad choices include an *ahi tataki* fresh tuna salad for $13, Southern fried chicken costs $8, and daily specials like Thursday's beef brisket run $8–14.

Saeng's

2119 Vineyard St ☎ 808/244-1567. Mon–Fri 11am–2.30pm & 5–9.30pm, Sat & Sun 5–9.30pm. Pleasant Thai restaurant, serving high-quality food at bargain prices. Plate lunches, on weekdays only, include honey-lemon chicken and garlic shrimp for $6–9, while selections from the full dinner menu cost a few dollars more.

A Saigon Cafe

1792 Main St ☎ 808/243-9560. Mon–Sat 10am–9.30pm, Sun 10am–8.30pm. Predominantly Vietnamese restaurant with an extremely wide-ranging and unusual menu, most of it very tasty. Hot and cold noodle dishes and soups, a lot of curries and seafood stew – even a "Vietnamese bouillabaisse" – plus simpler stir-fried and steamed fish specials, and plenty of vegetarian options. A filling noodle dish costs under $10, though some entrees range over $20, while appetizers like summer rolls and "Vietnamese burritos" are around $5. Even though its address is on Main Street, it's actually below the raised section of the highway, so you have to approach via Central Avenue.

Central Maui

Measuring just seven miles north to south, the verdant, narrow plains of central Maui, overshadowed by mighty Haleakalā to the east and the West Maui mountains to the west, are the island's economic heartland. Beyond the stunning 'Īao Valley, however, where ancient chiefs once ruled from a royal enclosure watered by four rivers, the rest of the isthmus was once a dry and relatively barren expanse. Only since sugar barons created irrigation channels to carry water from the eastern flanks of Haleakalā has the land been capable of supporting the agriculture that now makes it so green. In the northeast, the former sugar town of Pā'ia makes an attractive stop-off, offering good dining and shopping, while Mā'alaea in the southwest holds the popular Maui Ocean Center aquarium.

Tropical Gardens of Maui

'Īao Valley Road. Daily 9am–5pm; free. Spread away below and to the right of 'Īao Valley Road less than a mile west of Wailuku (see p.77), the small, commercial Tropical Gardens of Maui display and sell a colorful assortment of tropical plants from all over the world and mail specimens to the continental US. These also hold a small snack bar.

▼ KEPANIWAI COUNTY PARK

Kepaniwai County Park

'Īao Valley Road. Daily dawn–dusk; free. An attractive public garden set amid dramatic, curtain-like folds in the mountains, Kepaniwai County Park's lawns and flowerbeds are laid out in themed areas that pay tribute to Maui's Japanese, Chinese, and Portuguese immigrants, among others. Wandering the serene grounds you'll come upon a traditional thatched *hale*, ornamental pavilions and miniature pagodas, as well as statues of anonymous sugar-cane workers and even Doctor Sun Yat Sen.

Hawaii Nature Center

'Īao Valley Road. ☎808/244-6500, ⓦ www.hawaiinaturecenter.org. Daily 10am–4pm; $6, ages 8–12 $4. Largely an educational facility for schoolchildren, the Hawaii Nature Center, immediately adjoining Kepaniwai County Park, holds simple exhibitions on Hawaiian flora, fauna, and handicrafts. In addition, however, staff members conduct

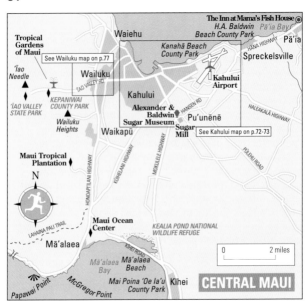

Tropical Gardens of Maui

'Iao Needle

'IAO VALLEY STATE PARK

KEPANIWAI COUNTY PARK

Wailuku Heights

See Wailuku map on p.77

Waiehu

Waikapū

Maui Tropical Plantation

N

LAHAINA PALI TRAIL

Mā'alaea

Papawai Point

McGregor Point

Mā'alaea Bay

Mai Poina 'Oe Ia'u County Park

Mā'alaea Beach

Maui Ocean Center

KEALIA POND NATIONAL WILDLIFE REFUGE

KIHEI ROAD

Kīhei

Wailuku

'IAO VALLEY RD

Kahului

HONOAPIILANI HIGHWAY

KUIHELANI HIGHWAY

MOKULELE HIGHWAY

Alexander & Baldwin Sugar Museum

Sugar Mill

Pu'unēnē

HANSEN RD

See Kahului map on p.72-73

Kanahā Beach County Park

Kahului Airport

HANA HIGHWAY

HALEAKALĀ HIGHWAY

PULEHU ROAD

The Inn at Mama's Fish House

H.A. Baldwin Beach County Park

Pa'ia Bay

Pā'ia

Spreckelsville

0   2 miles

CENTRAL MAUI

recommended guided hikes in the 'Iao Valley area (Mon–Fri 11.30am & 1.30pm, Sat & Sun 11am & 2pm; adults \$30, ages 8–12 \$20). As the high-mountain trails are otherwise closed to visitors, these provide the only access into the spectacularly lush wilderness that lies beyond the 'Iao Needle. The cost of the hikes includes admission to the center and a souvenir T-shirt.

'Iao Valley State Park

Daily 7am–7pm; free. 'Iao Valley Road – 'Iao is pronounced *ee-ow* – meanders to a dead end three miles west out of Wailuku, at the parking lot for 'Iao Valley State Park, which in all truth is more of a viewpoint than a park in its own right. Straight ahead, you're confronted by the spectacle of the 'Iao Needle, a 1200-foot pinnacle of green-clad lava that's one of Hawaii's

most famous natural spectacles. A short but steep footpath crosses 'Iao Stream and climbs up a nearby knoll for even better views from a covered rain shelter.

Despite appearances, the velvety Needle is not freestanding, but simply a raised knob at the end of a sinuous ridge. Towering, head usually in the clouds, at the intersection of two lush valleys, it's what geologists call an "erosional residual" – a nugget of hard volcanic rock left behind when the softer surrounding rocks were eroded away. The ancient Hawaiians, with their usual scatological gusto, named it Kuka'emoku, which politely translates as "broken excreta."

This whole area owes its existence to the phenomenal amount of rain that falls on West Maui; the 5788-foot peak of Pu'u Kukui, just over two miles from here, receives more than four hundred inches per year.

Unless you come early in the morning, it's likely to be raining in 'Īao Valley, but even when it's pouring you can usually look straight back down the valley to see the dry sunlit plains.

Following a series of accidents, the trails that lead beyond 'Īao Needle are closed to casual visitors, and can only be explored on the guided hikes run by the Hawaii Nature Center (see p.83). Climbing the Needle itself is a physical impossibility, owing to the crumbly nature of the rock.

However, two very short trails, paved but potentially slippery, loop down to 'Īao Stream from the main footpath, one on either side of the stream. Gardens laid out with native plants line the one closer to the parking lot, and the small waterlogged *lo'i* or taro patch here, similar to a paddy field, offers one of the best angles for photographs, as you look up past the footbridge towards the Needle itself.

Maui Tropical Plantation

1670 Honoapi'ilani Hwy, Waikapū. ℡ 808/244-7643, ⓦ www .mauitropicalplantation.com. Daily 9am–5pm, free; tram tours daily 10am–4pm, every 45min, $9.50, ages 3–12 $3.50. Though the

▲ 'ĪAO VALLEY STATE PARK

Maui Tropical Plantation, two miles south of Wailuku below the entrance to Waikapū Valley, is a principal stop on round-island bus tours, it's ultimately of minimal interest. Visitors are free to walk into the main "Marketplace," where the stalls are piled with plants, fruits, and souvenirs, and then pass into the lackluster gardens beyond to explore pavilions describing the cultivation of macadamia nuts, sugar, coffee, and other local crops. You can see a few more unusual plants on forty-minute tram tours, then take in the spectacular orchids in the nursery before you leave. The indoor *Tropical Restaurant*

The Battle of 'Īao Valley

For ancient Hawaiians, the gorgeous 'Īao Valley was the equivalent of Egypt's Valley of the Kings: they buried their royal dead in the long-lost Olopio cave, and access was barred to commoners. In 1790 the valley also came to be the final resting place for Maui warriors defeated by Kamehameha the Great, from the Big Island, in one of the many battles through which he eventually conquered the entire archipelago. Driven back from the shoreline by Kamehameha's fleet of war canoes, the local armies retreated into the valley, where they were bombarded with impunity by the great cannon *Lopaka*, directed by John Young and Isaac Davis (box p.54). While the defeated general, Kalanikupule, the son of Maui's chief Kahekili, fled across the mountains, the corpses of his men choked 'Īao Stream. Hence the name by which the battle became known – Kepaniwai, "the water dam."

serves unremarkable buffet lunches between 11am and 2pm (expect long lines), and sandwiches and salads the rest of the day.

Māʻalaea

At the point where Hwy-30 reaches the south coast, Māʻalaea, a former commercial port, has been given a new lease of life as the preferred marina of Maui's cruise and pleasure boats. The largest contingent are the Molokini snorkel boats (see p.177), which collectively bring Māʻalaea to life very early in the morning when the day's passengers assemble. This is al   an ideal time to catch great views of Haleakalā, whose summit pokes out above the ring of clouds that usually obscures it from Kīhei.

Swimming anywhere near Māʻalaea is not recommended, but there are good surfing breaks just to the south, while windsurfers hurtle out into Māʻalaea Bay from the thin and unexciting strip of sand

▼ MĀʻALAEA

The Lahaina Pali Trail

For an account of the Lahaina Pali Trail, which sets off across the southern tip of West Maui from just north of Māʻalaea, see p.55.

that stretches all the way east to Kīhei.

Maui Ocean Center

192 Māʻalaea Rd, Māʻalaea, ☎808/270-7000, ⓦwww .mauioceancenter.com. Sept–June daily 9am–5pm, July & Aug daily 9am–6pm, $23, ages 3–12 $16.
While Māʻalaea is not a town in any meaningful sense, it ˙ as acquired a center of sorts, in the form of the Māʻalaea Harbor Village mall. That in turn focuses on the Maui Ocean Center, a state-of-the-art aquarium providing a colorful introduction to the marine life of Hawaii. It's not quite as large as you might expect from the size of the entrance fee, but its exhibits are well chosen and very well displayed, and it has rapidly established itself as Maui's most visited paying attraction.

The most spectacular section comes first. The coral groves of the Living Reef (some of them fluorescent) hold such species as camouflaged scorpionfish, seahorses, octopuses, and bizarre "upside-down jellyfish." Eerie garden eels poke like blades of grass from the sandy seabed, but the star, of course, is the little *humuhumunukunukuapua'a* – literally, "the triggerfish with a snout like a pig."

Open-air terraces perched above the harbor hold tanks of huge rays and green sea turtles; as a rule, each turtle is kept at the aquarium for just a few months before being

▲ MAUI OCEAN CENTER

fitted with a tracking device and released into the ocean. Further on, additional displays cover the life cycle of whales, and the relationship between Hawaiians and the sea, including traditional fishing equipment. A final huge tank holds pelagic, or open-ocean, sea creatures; its walk-through glass tunnel means that you can stand beneath mighty sharks and rays as they swim above your head.

Certified scuba divers can arrange to take an accompanied dive into the tank for a one-on-one shark encounter (Mon, Wed & Fri 8.30am; $200); some divers have even been married in there.

Kealia Pond National Wildlife Refuge

Māʻalaea Bay, ☎808/875-1582. Free. Set back from Māʻalaea Bay and, for most of its length, Hwy-31, brackish Kealia Pond provides a haven for Hawaiian waterbirds as well as migratory species. Seldom more than two feet deep, and varying seasonally in size between around four hundred acres in winter and two hundred in summer, it's a rare enough remnant of Hawaiian wetlands that it's reserved as a wildlife refuge. Long boardwalks reach out across the water,

enabling visitors to watch birds like the *aeʻo* or Hawaiian stilt, and the native Hawaiian duck, *koloa maoli*.

Pāʻia

The friendly, laid-back town of Pāʻia, four miles east of Kahului on the Hāna Highway, is divided into two distinct sections, both of which began life serving the sugar plantations in the 1870s. Upper Pāʻia, concentrated around the sugar mill half a mile inland, was built on plantation land and held the camps that housed the laborers, as well as company stores and other facilities. Meanwhile, freebooting entrepreneurs set up shop in Lower Pāʻia, at sea level, operating stores, theaters, restaurants, and anything else that might persuade their captive clientele to part with a few pennies.

Both parts of Pāʻia declined apace with the collapse of agriculture, especially after the post-World War II drift to Kahului. The name "Pāʻia" today refers almost exclusively to what used to be Lower Pāʻia, which has re-emerged in recent years as a center for windsurfers and beach bums. The paint-peeling wooden buildings around the bottom end of Baldwin Avenue give it a very similar feel to Makawao, at the top of the road, while its role as the gateway to the Hāna Highway, coverage of which begins on p.126, keeps its gift stores and galleries busy with browsing tourists.

H.A. Baldwin Beach County Park

Narrow footpaths thread their way towards the ocean from central Pā'ia, passing between ramshackle houses with colorful gardens, to reach a short, tree-lined and sandy beach. Swimming here in Pā'ia Bay is rarely appealing, thanks to shallow, murky water and abundant seaweed, so locals head instead to the H.A. Baldwin Beach County Park, a mile west. Named after Harry Baldwin, son of Henry Baldwin of Alexander & Baldwin fame (see p.75), this was once the official sugar-company beach, and the chimneys of the sugar mill, which closed down in 2000, remain visible for the moment a few hundred yards off the highway, across the still-active cane fields. The beach itself is reached by a short approach road lined by a graceful curve of palm trees. Perfect bodysurfing waves crash onto its long unprotected stretch of sand, with safer swimming areas at either end.

Shops

Alice in Hulaland

19 Baldwin Ave, Pā'ia ☎ 808/579-9922. By far the best store on Maui for *tiki*-themed gifts and novelties, Alice in Hulaland is the place to go to pick up all those souvenirs that you'll otherwise kick yourself for not buying, from ceramic hula maidens to hi-ball glasses and cheap oilcloth decorated with Hawaiian motifs.

Nā Kani O Hula

110 Hāna Hwy at Baldwin Ave, Pā'ia ☎ 808/573-6332, ⓦ www.nakaniohula .com. Exceptional and unusual store-cum-crafts studio where Gayle Miyaguchi and Kent Apo make and sell authentic hula instruments and accessories, including *'ulī 'ulī* gourd rattles decorated with colorful feathers, as well as woven *lau hala* mats, hats, and bags.

▲ H.A. BALDWIN BEACH COUNTY PARK

▲ MĀ'ALAEA GRILL

Cafés

Anthony's Coffee Co

90C Hāna Hwy, Pā'ia ☎808/579-8340. Daily 5.30am–6pm. Small, early-opening coffee bar just west of central Pā'ia, fitted with a churning coffee roaster and serving espressos, pastries, soups, bagels, and deli sandwiches at a handful of indoor tables, plus $5 smoothies and a wide range of ice creams to go.

Restaurants

Cafe Mambo

30 Baldwin Ave, Pā'ia ☎808/579-8021. Daily 8am–9pm. Pale orange diner, just off the highway, serving espressos plus $6.50–9.50 burger or sandwich lunches and $9–19 dinner-time fajita specials. Picnics to go cost from $8.50 per person, $15 for two.

The Flatbread Company

89 Hāna Hwy, Pā'ia ☎808/579-8989. Daily 11.30am–10pm. If you suspect "flatbread" is a fancy way of saying "pizza," you're dead right. Call them what you will, these ones, cooked in a prominently positioned wood-fired clay oven, are delicious, courtesy of a small New England-based chain that places its emphasis on free range and organic ingredients. The restaurant itself is lively but unhurried. Twelve-inchers cost $9–11.50, and toppings include *kālua* pork and mango BBQ.

Fresh Mint

115 Baldwin Ave, Pā'ia ☎808/579-9144. Daily 11am–9pm. Smart, even cool, vegetarian Vietnamese restaurant. Lots of delicious noodles, stir-fries, soups, or curries, some with soy chicken or soy fish, others with tofu or just eggplants. All entrees cost around $10.

Mā'alaea Grill

Mā'alaea Harbor Village, 192 Mā'alaea Rd, Mā'alaea ☎808/243-2206. Mon 10.30am–5pm, Tues–Sun 10.30am–9pm. Perched above the harbor at the seaward end of Mā'alaea's central mall, with an ocean-view terrace that comes into its own at lunchtime, the *Mā'alaea Grill* serves conventional meat and seafood entrees at reasonable prices – reckon on $20 or less for a dinner entree – and specializes in salads at midday.

Māʻalaea Waterfront Restaurant

50 Hauʻoli St, Māʻalaea ☎808/244-9028. Daily 5–9.30pm; last seating 8.30pm. High-class dinner-only restaurant, in a somewhat hard-to-find location; to find it, head east – further around the bay – from the Maui Ocean Center. The menu focuses on expensive, freshly caught fish, with a cioppino stew priced at $38. The views are tremendous.

Mama's Fish House

799 Poho Place, Pāʻia ☎808/579-8488. Daily 11am–9pm. Upmarket and wildly popular fish restaurant, in breezy beachfront gardens a mile east of downtown Pāʻia. At lunch, you can opt for fish sandwiches and burgers for around $12, or go for full-scale fish entrees, each identified with the name of the fisherman who caught it. Dinner offers similar choices, along with even more fancy gourmet-Hawaiian dishes like *mahimahi* steamed in a *ti* leaf with coconut milk, costing anything from $30 upwards. While the views are sublime, if you come after sunset you may feel you're paying premium prices for little added value.

Milagros

112 Hāna Hwy at Baldwin Ave, Pāʻia ☎808/579-8755. Daily 8am–10pm. Friendly terrace café, serving all meals at parasol-shaded tables at Pāʻia's main intersection. Salads and deli sandwiches for around $8; burgers, tacos, and burritos for more like $10.

▲ PĀʻIA FISH MARKET

Moana Bakery & Cafe

71 Baldwin Ave, Pāʻia ☎808/579-9999. Daily 8am–9pm. Smart, tasteful café/restaurant not far off the main highway, with mosaic tables and large windows. Fancy breakfasts, lunchtime *saimin* or sandwiches ($7–10), and dinner entrees ($14–29) that range from green or red Thai curries to chili-seared *ahi* and *opakapaka laulau* (snapper wrapped in *ti* leaves).

Pāʻia Fish Market

110 Hāna Hwy at Baldwin Ave, Pāʻia ☎808/579-8030. Daily 11am–9.30pm. Informal, inexpensive place with wooden benches, where fresh fish – sashimi or blackened – is $14, while scallops, shrimp, and calamari cost a bit more, and a fish or meat burger is just $8. Fish'n'chips is $10 for lunch, $12 for dinner. Pasta entrees include chicken ($15) and seafood ($16), and there's a sideline in quesadillas, fajitas, and soft tacos.

Kīhei

If you've always thought of Hawaii as Condo Hell, then Kīhei probably comes closer to matching that image than anywhere else in the state. Stretching for seven miles south from Māʻalaea Bay in the region universally known as South Maui, it's a totally formless sprawl of a place, whose only landmarks consist of one dull mall or condo building after another. That said, it can be a perfectly pleasant place to spend your vacation, with abundant inexpensive lodging and dining options. It also holds plentiful beaches; each successive bay is filled with a narrow strip of white sand, so most hotels are within easy walking distance of a good stretch of beach. Just don't come to Kīhei expecting a town in any sense of the word; indeed, if you're staying anywhere else on the island, there's really no need to visit Kīhei at all.

Mai Poina ʻOe Iaʻu Beach County Park

The first easy point of access to the ocean along South Kīhei Road comes within a few hundred yards, at Mai Poina ʻOe Iaʻu Beach County Park. This narrow, shadeless beach is not somewhere you'd choose to spend a day, or to go swimming, but it's a good launching point for surfers, kayakers, and especially windsurfers. Māʻalaea Bay offers ideal conditions for relatively inexperienced windsurfers – and, for that matter, makes a good place for proficient sailboarders who are new to Hawaii to test the waters before venturing out into the mighty waves of Hoʻokipa (see p.126).

▲ MAI POINA ʻOE IAʻU BEACH COUNTY PARK

KĪHEI

Ōhukai Road

Mai Poina ʻOe La ʻu
Beach County Park

Hawaiian Islands
Humpback Whale NMS

Kō ʻie ʻie Fishpond

Kenolio Rd

Kaonoulu Rd

Kulanihakoʻi Street

Piʻilani Highway

Waipuʻilani Rd

Liloa Drive

ʻIliʻili Rd

Longs Center

Piʻikea Ave

Azeka Mauka

Piʻilani Village

Azeka Makai

Lipoa Street

Halekuai St

Māʻalaea Bay

Welekahao Road

South Kīhei Road

Halama St

Kukui Mall
Kīhei Town Center

Kīhei Kalama Village

Kalama Beach

Kanani Rd

Auhana Road

Alanui Ke Aliʻi Rd

Kamaʻole Beach
County Park 1

Dolphin Plaza
Kamaʻole Beach Center
Rainbow Mall
Kamaʻole Shopping Center

Kamaʻole Beach
County Park 2

Keonekai Road

Kamaʻole Beach
County Park 3

Kaiphale St

Kilohana

Kauhale Drive

Okolani Drive

Keawakapu
Beach Park

N

| 0 | Mile | 1 |

ACCOMMODATION

Aloha Pualani Hotel Boutique	A
Hale Kai Oʻkīhei	D
Kamaʻole Nalu Resort	H
Kīhei Akahi	I
Mana Kai Maui	J
Maui Coast Hotel	F
Maui Vista	E
Royal Mauian Resort	G
Sunseeker Resort	B
Wailana Inn	C

CAFÉS & RESTAURANTS

Azeka's	2
Canton Chef	6
The Coffee Store	3
Cyberbean	4
Five Palms Beach Grill	8
The Greek Bistro	7
Kīhei Caffe	5
Royal Thai	2
Roy's Kīhei Bar and Grill	1
Sansei Seafood Restaurant	4
Sarento's On The Beach	9
Stella Blues Café	3

Hawaiian Islands Humpback Whale National Marine Sanctuary

726 S Kīhei Rd, ☎808/879-2818 or 1-800/831-4888, ⊛www.hihwnms .nos.noaa.gov. Mon–Fri 10am–3pm; free. Squeezed onto a minor headland, not far south of Mai Poina ʻOe Iaʻu Beach at the northern end of Kīhei, a small compound serves as the headquarters of the Hawaiian Islands Humpback Whale National Marine Sanctuary. The organization was created to protect and study the estimated three thousand humpback whales that annually winter in Hawaiian waters. Enthusiastic volunteers can explain its work and talk you through the displays in the garage-like Education Center. Though the organization's offices, located in the larger blue house on the seafront,

are not open to the public, its spacious verandah is equipped with free binoculars and makes an ideal spot for watching whales in Māʻalaea Bay.

Kōʻieʻie Fishpond

A six-acre tract of ocean immediately offshore from the whale sanctuary headquarters is enclosed by the lava walls of the Kōʻieʻie Fishpond, which dates originally from the sixteenth century. The art of aquaculture, or fish-farming, was developed by the ancient Hawaiians to standards unmatched elsewhere in Polynesia. Such fishponds are laced around sheltered coastal areas on all the islands. The sea wall held one or two gaps, or sluice gates, which were usually sealed off with wooden lattices. Small fry could enter, but once they grew to full size they'd be unable to leave, and it was a simple matter to harvest them in nets. Saltwater fishponds like this one, used to raise ʻamaʻama (mullet) and awa (milkfish),

▲ KALAMA BEACH

were complemented by similar freshwater ponds, usually built near rivermouths that were sealed off from the sea by sandbars, and held such species as ʻōpae (shrimp) and ʻoʻopu (a native goby).

When this fishpond was constructed, the area was the site of the village of Kalepolepo. Its inhabitants left during the 1860s, after the fishpond became silted up due to runoff caused by the expansion of agriculture further up the slopes.

Kalama Beach

To the naked eye, and especially to guests staying at oceanfront properties such as the *Hale Kai O' Kīhei* and its neighbors (see p.162), the beaches of northern Kīhei look attractive enough, if rather narrow. However, thanks to the output of a sewage treatment facility here at Kalama Beach, this entire stretch is best admired from dry land; swimming is not recommended. Nonetheless, the large lawns and sports fields on the promontory at Kalama remain popular with locals, especially in the evenings, and there's a pretty coconut grove as well.

Kamaʻole Beach County Park

Much the busiest of the Kīhei beaches – and for good reason – are the three separate, numbered segments of Kamaʻole Beach County Park, immediately beyond Kalama. All boast clean white sand and are generally safe for swimming, with lifeguards and lovely views across the bay to West Maui. Most of beautifully soft Kamaʻole 1 beach is very close to the road, but it also curves away out of sight to the north, which is where you're likely to find the best snorkeling conditions. Little Kamaʻole 2, cradled between two headlands, is a bit short on shade, and very near a large concentration of condos, which leaves long, broad Kamaʻole 3 as the pick of the bunch. Families gather under the giant trees on its wide lawns, while the beach itself, which is especially popular with boogie-boarders, is shielded from the road at the bottom of a ten-foot grassy slope.

Keawakapu Beach Park

In high season, Keawakapu Beach Park, at the far south end of South Kīhei Road, makes a less crowded alternative to Kamaʻole. Swimming is best in the center, while there's good snorkeling off the rocks to the south, thanks to an artificial offshore reef made up mostly of old automobile parts that were submerged in the hope of boosting the local fish population.

Shops

Azeka Shopping Center

1279 & 1280 S Kīhei Rd. Matching pair of malls, the largest in Kīhei, standing across the main highway from each other. The older half, on the ocean side and also known as Azeka Makai, holds the local post office, a large Bank of Hawaii with ATMs, and several fast-food places, while the smarter Azeka Mauka section opposite offers more upscale eateries and a wide range of tourist oriented stores.

Beach Road Records

Rainbow Mall, 2439 S Kīhei Rd, ☏808/874-8863. Lots of secondhand as well as new CDs, and the expert advice willingly offered make Beach Road Records the best place to buy Hawaiian music on Maui; they stock other genres as well.

Hawaiian Moons Natural Foods

Kamaʻole Beach Center, 2411 S Kīhei Rd, ☏808/875-4356. Very good wholefood store with a great deli counter, and lots of high-quality cosmetics and beauty products, including island-made sunblocks, soaps, and oils.

Kīhei Kalama Village

1945 S Kīhei Rd. Several inexpensive restaurants-cum-bars-cum-fast-food outlets and a few tourist-oriented souvenir, T-shirt and aloha wear shops, comprise most of what this low-slung, open-air mall has on offer. In its central arcade of crafts and trinket stalls, you'll find some interesting creations by local Maui wood carvers, jewelers, ceramicists, and the like.

Cafés

The Coffee Store

Azeka Mauka, 1279 S Kīhei Rd ☏808/875-4244, ⓦwww.mauicoffee .com. Mon–Sat 6am–7pm, Sun 6am–5pm. Cheery mall café serving espressos of all kinds, plus breakfast pastries, lunch salads, pizzas, and sandwiches.

Cyberbean

Kīhei Town Center, 1881 S Kīhei Rd ☏808/879-4799. Mon–Sat 7am–9pm, Sun 8am–8pm. Internet café that, as well as specialty coffees, provides the usual array of inexpensive pizzas, salads, and sandwiches.

▲ KĪHEI CAFFE

Kīhei Caffe

1945 S Kīhei Rd ☎808/879-2230.
Daily 5am–3pm. Ramshackle
but friendly café offering
espressos, flavored lattes, and
smoothies, plus breakfast eggs
and pancakes and $8 lunchtime
sandwiches or burgers, to take
out or eat at a shaded roadside
gazebo.

Restaurants

Azeka's

Azeka Makai, 1280 S Kīhei Rd
☎808/879-0611. Daily 7.30am–5pm.
Small "local-style" snack shop
and takeout joint, with a few
tables, serving *saimin* ($3.50),
plus sushi and the Hawaiian
favorite *loco moco*, an egg-
topped hamburger. They
also sell marinated ribs, and
teriyaki beef and chicken,
all uncooked and ready for
barbecuing; in fact, in the
afternoon, they're the only
things available.

Canton Chef

Kama'ole Shopping Center, 2463
S Kīhei Rd ☎808/879-1988. Daily
11am–2pm & 5–9pm. Roomy
Chinese restaurant, with $8
lunch specials and a dinner
menu bursting with chicken,
shrimp, scallop, and fish entrees
($8–22), including several served
in a tangy black-bean sauce.
With advance notice, they'll
prepare a whole Peking duck
for $42.50.

Five Palms Beach Grill

Mana Kai Maui, 2960 S Kīhei Rd
☎808/879-2607. Daily 8am–9.30pm.
Beachfront restaurant in a
spectacular setting on the
ground floor of a condo
building, with open terraces
within earshot of the waves,
and live music nightly. An *à la
carte* brunch menu is
served until 2.30pm daily,
including a seared-tuna eggs
Benedict for $18, or salad or
lunch specials for $13–20.
Dinner items – mostly Pacific
Rim, along with standard ribs
and steaks – are delicious and
beautifully presented, with
appetizers such as soft-shell
crab cakes in Japanese tartare
sauce ($16) and entrees like
fresh *opah* (moonfish), and
Szechuan glazed rack of lamb
($28–43).

▲ FIVE PALMS BEACH GRILL

The Greek Bistro

2511 S Kīhei Rd ☏ 808/879-9330. Daily 5–10pm. Friendly, dinner-only Greek place on a garden terrace set back from the road and crammed with coconut palms and a banyan tree. The food is OK without being wonderful, but makes a welcome and potentially healthy change. Appetizers like feta and olive salad, or stuffed grape leaves go for $8–12; entrees include *moussaka* and *souvlaki* for under $20, while a mixed platter costs $25 per person.

Roy's Kīhei Bar and Grill

Pi'ilani Village, 303 Pi'ikea Ave ☏ 808/891-1120. Daily 5.30–10pm. Large, always busy and very highly recommended dinner-only outlet of the upscale island chain, beside the upper highway in a mall half a mile up from Kīhei Road. Signature Roy's dishes such as lemongrass-crusted *shutome* (swordfish) and blackened rare *ahi* stream from the open kitchen, at around $10–13 for an appetizer and $25–30 for an entree. The steamed fresh catch ($30) is irresistible, while half a Mongolian roasted duck or honey-mustard short ribs is $26. Rather than bread, they provide a dish of *edamame* beans. A three-course set menu costs $40.

Royal Thai

Azeka Makai, 1280 S Kīhei Rd ☏ 808/874-0813. Mon–Fri 11am–3pm & 4.45–9.30pm, Sat & Sun 4.45–9.30pm. Small place, tucked away at the back of the mall, serving Kīhei's best Thai food. Choose from red, yellow, and green curries in vegetarian, meat, and fish versions; *tom yum* (spicy and sour soup) and long-rice soups; and mussels in black-bean sauce – all for $8–12.

Sansei Seafood Restaurant

Kīhei Town Center, 1881 S Kīhei Rd ☏ 808/669-6286. Mon–Wed & Sun 5.30–10pm, Thurs–Sat 5.30pm–1am. Sensational Japanese–Hawaiian, dinner-only restaurant, also found in Kapalua (see p.70). Individual appetizers and entrees are invariably delicious, but the special Omakase Tasting Menu, at $68 for two, is fabulous value, offering copious portions of signature dishes such as *miso* butterfish and the Asian rock shrimp cake. It's all pretty hectic, so don't expect to linger over a romantic dinner, and there are no views, but it's a dynamic, even glamorous spot, and the food is out of this world. Laser karaoke until 2am at weekends.

Sarento's on the Beach

Best Western Oceanfront Inn, 2980 S Kīhei Rd ☎808/875-7555. Daily 5.30–10pm. This Italian restaurant, located at Kīhei's southern end in an open-sided pavilion adjoining Keawakapu Beach that is gently spotlit once the sun goes down, is very much a special-occasion kind of place. Everything is scrupulously tasteful, from the complimentary focaccia breads to the Sinatra soundtrack, but with starters like gazpacho with crab or the house salad costing $12–18, and entrees such as tiger shrimp at over $30, or *fra diavolo* seafood stew for $45, the check can be gargantuan, especially if you buy your souvenir photo from the house photographer.

Stella Blues Café

Azeka Mauka, 1279 S Kīhei Rd ☎808/874-3779. Daily 7.30am–10pm. California-style café, complete with ponytailed waiters and Grateful Dead posters, and centering on a huge wood-burning grill. The menu includes continental and cooked breakfasts ($6–10); burger, salad, and sandwich lunches ($8–15; try the special of grilled and roasted vegetables on herb bread); dinners like fettuccini Alfredo, Cajun chicken, crab cakes, and ribs ($15–24); as well as an assortment of smoothies and espressos.

▲ SANSEI SEAFOOD RESTAURANT

Wailea and Mākena

With South Maui's finest beaches and most attractive landscapes, it's by no coincidence that the resort area of Wailea and Mākena is much more exclusive and upscale than what's found further north at Kīhei. Bracketed between the velvet lawns of the golf courses that carpet the higher slopes inland, and crescent beaches of white sand along the seashore, Wailea and Mākena together are dominated by half a dozen large and luxurious properties. Each is a fully-fledged fantasyland containing hundreds of rooms, several restaurants and shops, vast landscaped complexes of pools and gardens, and additional amenities like spas and tennis courts. What the resorts don't have, however, are their own private beaches; here, like everywhere else in Hawaii, the beaches are public. Glorious strands like Polo and Maluaka should not be missed, while resort development stops just short of the best beach of all, Oneloa or Big Beach. The coastal highway peters out not far beyond at secluded La Pérouse Bay, one of the island's the finest snorkeling and kayaking destinations.

Ulua Beach

The northernmost access to Wailea's beaches is provided by a short road that leads from just past the *Renaissance Wailea* down to Ulua Beach. As this stretch of coast usually experiences the highest surf in South Maui, the beach is popular with body-surfers and boogie-boarders. There's also great snorkeling around the rocky point that

separates it from Mōkapu Beach, a short walk to the north.

Wailea Beach

Although Wailea Beach itself, reached by a spur road between the *Grand Wailea* and the *Four Seasons*, is the most overshadowed by the resorts of all the beaches in the vicinity, the hotels are here for a reason. A broad, magnificent expanse

▼ WAILEA BEACH

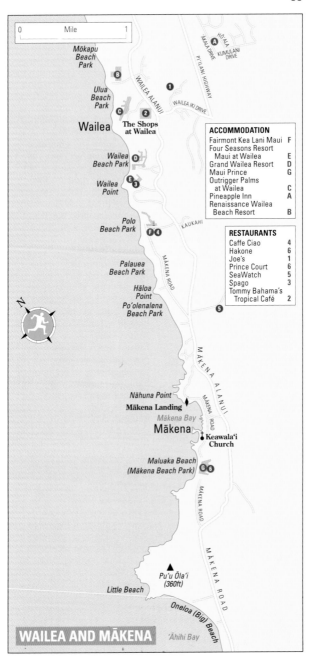

ACCOMMODATION

Fairmont Kea Lani Maui	F
Four Seasons Resort Maui at Wailea	E
Grand Wailea Resort	D G
Maui Prince	G
Outrigger Palms at Wailea	C
Pineapple Inn	A
Renaissance Wailea Beach Resort	B

RESTAURANTS

Caffe Ciao	4
Hakone	6
Joe's	1
Prince Court	6
SeaWatch	5
Spago	3
Tommy Bahama's Tropical Café	2

WAILEA AND MĀKENA

▲ POLO BEACH

old-fashioned swimming. A pleasant, paved coastal trail connects it to Wailea Beach, while if you're driving there's plenty of parking just off Kaukahi Street, on the south side of the *Fairmont Kea Lani*. The path down from the parking lot hits the sand at Polo Beach's northern end, which, being right beneath the hotel, can feel rather like a goldfish bowl, crammed with loungers and short on shade. Double back south, however, and you'll come to two much less crowded stretches, which in winter become distinct beaches.

of curving sand, it offers safe swimming virtually year round, with a gentle ripple at the southern end to please first-time boogie-boarders, and easy snorkeling around the rocks at either extremity. The views are great too, looking across the bay with its busy pleasure-boat traffic and whales in winter to East Maui on the far side.

Polo Beach

Polo Beach, immediately south of Wailea Beach, is the best of the lot for good

Palauea Beach

Well away from the built-up areas, Palauea Beach is the quietest of the Wailea beaches. Surfers and boogie-boarders predominate, but it's also a good spot for a family day by the sea, and for snorkeling. In 1994, Palauea Beach was where the US Navy held a ceremony formally handing control of the island of Kahoʻolawe, clearly visible out to sea, back to the people of Hawaii.

Mākena Bay

Mākena Road, which leaves Mākena Alanui Drive a little over

Kahoʻolawe

The uninhabited island of Kahoʻolawe is visible from all along Maui's south and west coasts, and especially around Wailea and Mākena. Measuring just eleven miles by six, and a maximum of 1477 feet above sea level, it's the eighth-largest Hawaiian island, with its nearest point a mere eight miles off Maui. From a distance, Kahoʻolawe looks like a barren hillock; at sunset it glows red, thanks to a haze of red dust lifted by the winds. Trapped in the rainshadow of Haleakalā, it receives thirty inches of rain a year. Agriculture is all but impossible, though a few green valleys, invisible from the other islands, cut into the central plateau.

During World War II, the island was appropriated by the US Navy, which used it to practice the kind of amphibious landings that ultimately ensured the defeat of Japan. After prolonged campaigning by Hawaiian activists, it was eventually handed back to the state of Hawaii in 1994. It's still, however, being cleared of unexploded ordnance, and access remains extremely restricted.

▲ KEAWALA'I CONGREGATIONAL CHURCH

a mile south of the *Kea Lani*, skirts the shoreline of Mākena Bay. This was once the site of busy Mākena Landing harbor, which was superseded by the creation of Kahului's new docks in the 1920s. The jetty has now gone, leaving behind a sleepy black-lava bay with little sand.

Keawala'i Congregational Church

Keawala'i Congregational Church stands on an oceanfront patch of lawn that doubles as a graveyard, surrounded by trees with multicolored blossoms. It's a plain cement structure, topped by a pretty, wood-shingled belfry, and painted with a neat green trim; the coconut palms beyond front a tiny beach. Visitors are welcome to the 7.30am and 10am Sunday services, which incorporate Hawaiian language and music.

Maluaka Beach

Keawala'i Church is opposite the parking lot for Maluaka Beach – also known as Mākena Beach Park, which naturally leads to confusion with Mākena State Park, described below – a hundred yards down the road. Though dominated somewhat by the *Maui Prince*, especially at its southern end, it remains an attractive little half-moon beach, with reasonable snorkeling. Its combination of relative tranquility and superb sunset views over to Molokini and Kaho'olawe also makes it a favorite spot for wedding ceremonies.

Oneloa Beach (Big Beach)

Maui's most spectacular sweep of golden sand stretches for over half a mile south of the landmark cinder cone of Pu'u 'Ōla'i, just south of Mākena. There's not a building in sight at Oneloa Beach (literally "long sand," and widely known as Big Beach), just perfect sands and mighty surf, backed by a dry forest of *kiawe* and cacti. During the 1970s, it was home to a short-lived hippy commune; nowadays it's officially Mākena State Park, with two paved access roads.

The very first turn off the main road south of Mākena, though labeled "Mākena State Park," is a dirt track that leads via an orange gate to a scrubby gray-sand beach. Instead, keep going on the main road until you reach the paved turnoff to Oneloa, three quarters of a mile beyond the *Maui Prince*. A footpath from the parking lot here leads through the trees to a small cluster of portable toilets and picnic tables, and then emerges at the north end of Big Beach. While the clear blue ocean across this broad expanse of deep, coarse sand is irresistible, Big Beach is actually extremely dangerous, because it faces straight out to sea and lacks a reef to protect it. Huge waves crash right onto the shoreline, and fearsome rip currents tear along the coast just a few feet out. Although it's been the scene of many drownings, all lifeguards were controversially withdrawn several years ago due to budget cuts.

Despite its perils, Big Beach remains busy most of the time with enthusiastic swimmers, boogie-boarders, and even snorkelers. Non-locals tend to congregate at its northern end, where in calmer periods the red-brown cliffs provide enough shelter to create a little turquoise "lagoon" of relatively placid water.

Little Beach

Walk right to the northern end of Big Beach, and, as if by magic, a natural cleft in the cliff reveals the "stairway" across the rocks that enables you to reach the much smaller, and significantly safer, Little Beach. Shielded by a rocky headland, and shaded by the adjacent trees, this is perhaps the most idyllic swimming spot on Maui, with views of Molokini and Lanai. The winter surf can still get pretty high, however, so it helps if you're into body-surfing.

One relic of the hippy days is that Little Beach is still widely known as an (illegal) nudist beach; even if you don't go naked yourself, some of your fellow beachgoers certainly will. As a result, they can be extremely sensitive to intruders carrying, let alone using, cameras.

Puʻu ʻŌlaʻi

Halfway along the easy trail between Big and Little beaches, where the ground levels off at the top of the first cliff, another trail doubles back to climb Puʻu ʻŌlaʻi itself. This crumbling cinder cone was produced by one of Maui's

The first foreigner on Maui

By spending three hours ashore at the bay that's now named after him, on May 30, 1786, French Admiral Jean-François Galaup, Comte de la Pérouse became the first foreigner to set foot on Maui. He was under orders to claim the island for the King of France but, unusually for a European, considered that he had no right to do so. His ships, the *Astrolabe* and the *Boussole*, simply sailed away, and were lost with all hands in the Solomon Islands two years later.

Before departing, La Pérouse encountered a handful of coastal villages in the area. Its inhabitants knew it as *Keoneʻōʻio*, or "bonefish beach," and told of how chief Kalaniʻopuʻu of the Big Island had landed a fleet of canoes here during an attempted invasion of Maui a few years earlier. However, the villages were largely destroyed just four years after La Pérouse's visit by the last known eruption of Haleakalā. A river of lava two miles wide flowed into the sea at the center of what had been one long bay, to create the two separate bays seen today. Look inland from here to see several russet cinder cones that are relics of the eruptions.

very last volcanic eruptions, perhaps two centuries ago, and is barely held together by scrubby grass and thorns. The ascent is so steep that strongly worded signs warn against making the attempt. If you do try, you may find you have to advance on all fours. Scrambling over the raw red – and very sharp – cinders is extremely painful in anything other than proper hiking boots.

The summit of Puʻu ʻŌlaʻi – which is not the peak you see at the start of the climb – is a wonderful vantage point for watching humpback whales in winter. It commands views all the way up the flat coast to Wailea and Kīhei, down the full length of Big Beach, inland to the green uplands of Haleakalā, across the ocean to the low ridge of Molokini – circled by cruise boats from dawn onwards – and beyond to glowing red Kahoʻolawe, the West Maui Mountains, and Lanai.

La Pérouse Bay

Mākena Road continues for another three miles south from Big Beach, as a narrow, undulating road that often narrows to a single lane. During the initial stretch, it runs right beside the ocean, clinging to the coastline of ʻĀhihi Bay around several small coves lined by very rough, jagged *ʻaʻā* lava, before setting out across a wide, desolate field of yet more chunky lava. La Pérouse Bay lies beyond. In theory, this southernmost point of Maui is the driest part of the island, which means it receives heavy traffic on those days when it seems to be raining everywhere else. That can make reaching it a long, slow process, with no guarantee that it won't be raining here too. Most visitors

▲ LA PÉROUSE BAY

either park or turn around at what looks like the end of the road, where a cairn bearing a bronze plaque commemorates the voyages of the French Admiral Jean-François Galaup, Comte de la Pérouse. In fact, however, you can turn right at the cairn and continue for another couple of hundred yards to the shoreline, where there's much more parking space.

Āhihi-Kīnaʻu Natural Area Reserve

The waters around the headland at the east end of La Pérouse Bay are set aside as the ʻĀhihi-Kīnaʻu Natural Area Reserve, notable for its large numbers of dolphins. All fishing is forbidden; snorkeling is allowed, but it's easier to enter the water in the inlets around La Pérouse Bay itself than to go in off the sharp rocks of the headland. The very best snorkeling areas can only be reached on foot, along a trail that follows the shoreline around to the right when you reach the end of the road, to a succession of successively clearer

▲ ĀHIHI-KĪNA'U NATURAL AREA RESERVE

little coves. Scuba divers too enter the water straight from the shore, most usually from 'Āhihi Bay. In addition, the kayak operators listed on p.177 run excursions here. The trail from the road meanders alternately across the sands and among the scrubby *kiawe* trees to follow the whole curve of the bay. The lichen-covered walls of ancient dwellings can often be glimpsed in the undergrowth.

Kanaio Beach

At the far end of La Pérouse Bay, you come to another field of crumbled, reddish-brown lava. A separate trail – not the obvious coastal path, which soon peters out, but one further inland – heads onwards from here. While it's of some historic interest, tracing the route of the King's Highway footpath that once ringed the entire island is extremely rugged, hot, and exposed. As archeologists and environmentalists alike are keen to minimize the impact of visitation on this area, it's probably best not to bother.

If you do decide to keep going, little-visited Kanaio Beach, a pretty cove of turquoise water two miles along, is as far as it makes any sense to go, and even that's not a hike to undertake lightly.

Shops

The Shops at Wailea

3750 Wailea Alanui Drive, Wailea ☎808/891-6770, ⓦwww .shopsatwailea.com. The proximity of so many big-spending tourists has ensured the rapid growth of the Shops at Wailea to become Maui's most upscale shopping

▼ SHOPS AT WAILEA

mall. Its ideal target audience can readily be divined from the presence of Louis Vuitton, Gucci, and Tiffany outlets, but it also holds plenty of stores aimed at more ordinary folk, including Honolua Surf Co for surf and aloha wear; Martin and MacArthur for top-notch Hawaiian crafts and playful tiki souvenirs; Footprints; Banana Republic; and a well-stocked Ritz Camera, the island's best camera store.

Restaurants

Caffe Ciao

Fairmont Kea Lani, 4100 Wailea Alanui Drive, Wailea ☎808/875-2225. Daily 6.30am–10pm. Very good, if pricey, Italian bakery/deli/ trattoria, downstairs and to the left of the *Kea Lani's* imposing lobby. The deli section sells pastries and espressos all day, plus massive sandwiches like a hummus wrap for $8.50 or a pesto sandwich for $9, while the trattoria serves more formal meals on an open-air terrace, with lunchtime panini or pasta specials for $14–20, and dinners ranging from $17–19 pizzas up to a veal *saltimbocca* for $31 or a $36 *cioppino* seafood stew.

Hakone

Maui Prince, 5400 Mākena Alanui Drive, Mākena ☎808/875-5888. Tues–Sat 6–9pm. Classic dinner-only Japanese restaurant, upstairs in the *Prince*, with tastefully minimal decor – but for the odd framed vintage *aloha* shirt – and no views. On Saturdays, there's a $45 dinner buffet; otherwise the seven-course Rakuen Kaiseki set menu costs $60, but you can also order sushi or sashimi dinners for around $40, smaller set menus for more like $35, or

▲ CAFFE CIAO

simply individual dishes from the sushi bar.

Joe's

131 Wailea Iki Place, Wailea ☎808/875-7767. Daily 5.30–9pm. One of Maui's most fashionable restaurants, owned by the same top-notch team as the *Hali'imaile General Store* (see p.113). Neither the tennis-club setting nor the decor – dull rock-music memorabilia – will grab you, but the food is heavenly, a fusion of cutting-edge Pacific Rim cuisine with down-home local favorites. Appetizers ($8–20) include *ahi* tartare with wasabi aioli, while entrees ($20 and up) range from meatloaf with garlic mashed potatoes to a smoky, applewood-grilled salmon.

Prince Court

Maui Prince, 5400 Mākena Alanui Drive, Mākena ☎808/875-5888. Mon–Sat 6–9pm, Sun 9am–1pm & 6–9pm. Relatively formal, somewhat solemn resort restaurant. Appetizers include oysters on the half-shell ($14), and a tower of Hawaiian tuna and *foie gras* ($14). Apart from fish dishes like the tempura *moi* (threadfish) for $28, the entrees tend to be rather predictable, though caramelized Maui onions lift options like roast lamb or venison. Sunday morning sees a buffet brunch, and Friday night a prime rib and seafood buffet; both cost $43.

SeaWatch

100 Wailea Golf Club Drive, Wailea ☎ 808/875-8080. Daily 8am–3pm & 5.30–9pm. Grand terrace restaurant in the clubhouse of the Wailea Golf Club, a few hundred yards uphill from the highway, open daily for all meals and enjoying stupendous ocean views during daylight hours. Lunch is the best time to come, with well-priced specials like the $9 *kālua* pork sandwich; at night the cuisine is Pacific Rim, with $8–15 appetizers such as five-spice crab cakes, and $26–36 entrees including fish, grilled chicken, and lamb with onion torte.

Spago

Four Seasons, 3900 Wailea Alanui Drive, Wailea ☎ 808/879-2999. Daily 5.30–9.30pm. Celebrity chef Wolfgang Puck spreads himself a little thin these days, but as befits the stunning ocean-view location in this grandest of resorts, the buzzy, glamorous *Spago* pulls out all the stops.

It serves dinner only, with an assured and irresistible Pacific-Rim menu that includes a great scallop *ceviche* with Kula onions ($23), delicious *ahi poke* (spicy cubes of raw tuna) served in sesame-miso cones ($18), and entrees like whole steamed *hapu'upu'u* (sea bass) for $40, or grilled lamb chops with chili-mint vinaigrette for $49.

Tommy Bahama's Tropical Café

The Shops at Wailea, 3750 Wailea Alanui Drive, Wailea ☎ 808/875-9983. Sun–Thurs 11am–11pm, Fri & Sat 11am–midnight. Pricey but pretty good bar and restaurant adjoining the upscale clothes store of the same name. At lunch, you can tuck into huge fishy sandwiches or pasta specials for $15–20 – try the tasty Habana Cubana barbecue pork sandwich – while enjoying sweeping (if distant) ocean views from the terrace. The dinner entrees are more overtly Caribbean, including a Port au Prince spiced pork chop ($35) and Trinidad tuna with cilantro and lemongrass ($40).

Shows

Maui Sunset Lū'au

Maui Prince, 5400 Mākena Alanui Drive, Mākena ☎ 808/875-5888. Tues & Thurs 5.30pm, $83. Although none of South Maui's *lū'aus* is as good as the Royal Lahaina Lū'au or the Feast at Lele in Lahaina – see p.58 – the expansive lawns of the *Maui Prince* make a great venue for an evening of eating Hawaiian foods, drinking cocktails, and watching – and even participating in – *hula* performances. The emphasis is more on partying than on presenting authentic Polynesian culture.

▼ MAUI SUNSET LŪ'AU

Upcountry Maui

The lower western slopes of Haleakalā, which enjoy a deliciously temperate climate a couple of thousand feet above the isthmus, are known as Upcountry Maui. Although most visitors, drawn onwards up the mountain, don't linger here, it's among the most attractive regions in all Hawaii, with lush orchards and rainforests around Makawao in the north giving way to the parched cattle country of 'Ulupalakua Ranch twenty miles to the south. It holds few significant towns and even fewer tourist attractions, and visitor accommodation is limited to a handful of small-scale B&Bs. Instead, the upcountry is marked by small farms-cum-gardens – particularly in the area of Kula – which are famous for their flowering plants, especially dazzling protea blossoms, and consistently superb views back over the isthmus, to the ocean and the West Maui Mountains.

Makawao

The small town of Makawao, seven miles up from coastal Pā'ia (see p.87), represents Maui at its best. Still recognizable as the village built by plantation workers and Hispanic *paniolo* cowboys in the nineteenth century, it's now home to an active artistic community dominated by exiles from California. When they're not giving each other classes in yoga, feng shui, belly dancing, and Hawaiian healing, they make its galleries, crafts stores, and coffee bars some of the liveliest hangouts on the island.

Although Makawao extends for well over a mile, only its central intersection – where Baldwin Avenue, climbing from Pā'ia, meets Makawao Avenue from Pukalani – holds any great interest. Baldwin here points straight up Haleakalā, drawing the eye towards the lush green meadows on the slopes above town. Its timber-frame buildings, painted in fading pastel hues, are connected by a rudimentary boardwalk and hold half a dozen quirky art galleries. The real artistic epicenter of town, however, is the Hui No'eau Visual Arts Center, a country estate a mile south at 2841 Baldwin Ave (Mon–Sat 10am–4pm; ☎808/572-6560, Ⓦwww.huinoeau.com). As well as offering classes in practical

▼ MAKAWAO

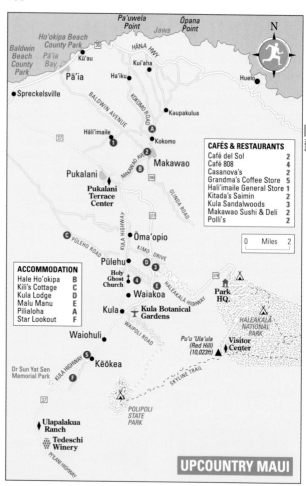

CAFÉS & RESTAURANTS

Café del Sol	2
Café 808	4
Casanova's	2
Grandma's Coffee Store	5
Hali'imaile General Store	1
Kitada's Saimin	3
Kula Sandalwoods	3
Makawao Sushi & Deli	2
Polli's	2

ACCOMMODATION

Hale Ho'okipa	B
Kili's Cottage	C
Kula Lodge	D
Malu Manu	E
Pilialoha	A
Star Lookout	F

UPCOUNTRY MAUI

arts and crafts, it houses its own small store and a gallery for temporary exhibitions.

Makawao's *paniolo* heritage is commemorated on July 4 each year by the Makawao Rodeo, which includes a parade through town as well as competitive events at the Oskie Rice Arena.

Pukalani

The shapeless sprawl known as Pukalani is home to six thousand people, but has no appreciable downtown area. As a bypass now carries traffic around rather than through it, there's no real reason for tourists ever to see the town at all. However, the run-down Pukalani Terrace Center mall holds the closest gas station to the summit of Haleakalā, as well as a big Foodland supermarket, a *Subway* sandwich shop, and several budget diners.

Holy Ghost Church

Five miles south of the point where it branches away from the route up to Haleakalā, the lower upcountry road, the Kula Highway, passes just below the white octagonal Holy Ghost Church. Portuguese Catholics came to Maui from 1878 onwards, and by 1894 were prosperous enough to construct their own church, shipping the hand-carved high-relief gilt altar from Austria, and capping the structure with a gleaming silver-roofed belfry. The interior is very light, with pink-painted walls, and features the Stations of the Cross labeled in Portuguese. Not surprisingly, this was the only octagonal structure built in nineteenth-century Hawaii; it's thought to be eight-sided either because the crown of the Portuguese Queen Isabella was octagonal, or because the German parish priest came from near Aachen, the site of a similar octagonal chapel built by Charlemagne.

Kula Botanical Garden

638 Kekaulike Hwy, Kula ☎ 808/878 1715. Daily 9am–4pm; $5, kids 6–12 $1. A couple of miles beyond the foot of Haleakalā Crater Road, the Kula Botanical Garden offers enjoyable self-guided tours through large and colorful landscaped gardens. Among its broad range of plants are proteas, hydrangeas, lurid yellow and red canna, and spectacular purple and yellow birds of paradise from South Africa. Many of the plant species betray their Pacific origins by bearing the Latin name *banksia*, in honor of Sir Joseph Banks, the pioneering botanist who sailed with Captain Cook; perhaps the finest is the red and white "Raspberry Frost" from Australia.

Polipoli State Park

Although Maui residents rave about thickly wooded Polipoli State Park, set high above the upcountry, visitors from beyond Hawaii may feel that as an "ordinary" temperate forest it holds little they can't see at home. That said, the drive up is fun, taking you off the beaten track into Maui's remoter reaches.

▲ HOLY GHOST CHURCH

Due to a major forest fire, Polipoli Park had to be closed for six months in the first half of 2007. Although it has since re-opened, it remains visibly scarred, and not all of its dirt roads and trails were passable at the time this book went to press. Check locally before you visit.

Polipoli Park stands at the top of the ten-mile Waipoli Road – *not* nearby Polipoli Road, oddly enough – which climbs away from Kekaulike Highway just south of the Kula Botanical Garden. The first six miles, in which you do all the climbing, are paved, passing through tough, springy ranchland where cattle graze on the open range. This is Maui's best launching spot for hang-gliders, which you may see sharing the winds with circling Hawaiian owls (rare among owls in that they fly by day, rather than night).

It shouldn't be too difficult to coax a rental car along the rough, but level, dirt road that meanders along the hillside above the ranch. After three miles, the road surface improves; drop right at the fork half a mile further along, and after another half a mile you'll come to Polipoli's campground in a grassy clearing, which offers neither showers nor drinking water. Tent camping here ($5), and overnight stays in the simple cabin nearby ($45 for up to four people; closed Tues), can be arranged through the state parks office in Wailuku (see p.166).

The entire Polipoli area was planted with Californian redwood trees by the Civilian Conservation Corps during the 1930s. The Redwood Trail, which leads down from a hundred yards before the campground, burrows through such thick forest that the persistent rain can barely penetrate it, and very little light does either. The forest floor is too gloomy even to support a light scattering of moss, and many of the tightly packed trees are dead. It comes as a huge relief when the trail emerges from the bottom-most strip of eucalyptus after 1.5 miles to show expansive views across the ranchlands.

The Skyline Trail

Various other trails crisscross throughout Polipoli, including some to lava caves hidden in the woods, but the only one

▼ POLIPOLI STATE PARK

likely to interest visitors from outside Hawaii is the Skyline Trail. This epic thirteen-mile trek follows the southwest rift zone of Haleakalā right the way up to Science City, at the summit (see p.120); it too was closed following the 2007 fire, so check with the park service if you're hoping to make the hike. It climbs a dirt track that heads off to the left two miles along the left fork from the junction 9.5 miles up Waipoli Road, described above. Unless you arrange a pickup at the far end, it's too far for a day-hike, and the higher you get the more exposed to the biting winds you'll be. Alternatively, you can take a mountain bike along the trail.

Keōkea

A couple of miles south of the intersection of the Kekaulike and Kula highways, the village of Keōkea consists of a small cluster of roadside stores, together with the green and white St John's Episcopal Church. All were built at the end of the nineteenth century to serve the local Chinese community, which also supported three Chinese-language schools and, it's said, a number of opium dens. Alongside *Grandma's Coffee Store* (see p.113), one room of Henry Fong's general store houses the appealing little Keokea Gallery (Tues–Sat 9am–5pm, Sun 9am–3pm), where you'll find arts and crafts displayed.

The wife and children of Sun Yat Sen, the first President of China, stayed on his brother's ranch here during 1911 and 1912, while Sun was away fomenting revolution. Hence the statue of Sun, guarded by Chinese dragons, that looks out over Wailea and Kahoolawe

from the somewhat neglected Dr Sun Yat Sen Memorial Park, which lies at the intersection of Hwy-37 and Kealakapu Road, less than two miles beyond Keōkea.

Thanks to its healthy elevation, Keōkea was also the site of Kula Sanatorium, which opened in 1910 to treat tuberculosis sufferers, and was soon joined by a "Preventorium" that set out to reduce the incidence of the disease.

'Ulupalakua Ranch

Six miles on from Keokea, the six tin-roofed, single-story wooden buildings of the 'Ulupalakua Ranch headquarters nestle into a shady bend in the road. Comings and goings are overseen by the three carved wooden cowboys stationed permanently on the porch of the 'Ulupalakua Ranch Store (daily 9am–4.30pm); inside, you can buy simple lunches, including burgers made from the ranch's own cattle, plus *paniolo* hats, T-shirts, and limited basic supplies.

'Ulupalakua Ranch started out in the middle of the nineteenth century as Rose Ranch, owned by an ex-whaling captain, James McKee. Originally its main business was sugar, but the focus soon shifted to cattle, and it employed expert *paniolo* cowboys such as Ike Purdy, a former world rodeo champion. In his huge mansion, McKee played host to Robert Louis Stevenson and King David Kalākaua among others, who took advantage of Hawaii's first ever swimming pool. Spotting ships arriving at Mākena Landing (see p.100), McKee would fire a cannon to signal that he was sending a carriage down to meet his guests. The

▲ TEDESCHI WINERY

mansion burned down during the 1970s, but the ranch itself is still going, raising elk and sheep as well as cattle.

Tedeschi Winery

Kula Hwy, 'Ulupalakua ☏ 877/878-6058, ⊛ www.mauiwine.com. Store and museum daily 9am–5pm, free tours daily 10.30am, 1.30pm & 3pm. Around the corner from 'Ulupalakua Ranch, one of the ranch's co-owners has established the Tedeschi Winery as a successful sideline on the site of James McKee's original Rose Ranch. It uses two annual grape harvests from a small vineyard in a fold below the highway, a mile to the north, to produce 30,000 cases a year of white, red, and rosé wines, as well as *Maui Brut* champagne and sweet, dry and even sparkling pineapple wines. They're on sale in the King's Cottage, which also houses an entertaining little museum of ranch and cowboy history and serves as the assembly point for fifteen-minute guided tours. The converted and imitation ranch buildings used for processing and bottling are less than enthralling, but you do at least get to see

some amazing trees, including a pine drowning in multicolored creeping bougainvillea, and a giant camphor.

Pi'ilani Highway

South of 'Ulupalakua, Kula Highway confusingly becomes the Pi'ilani Highway, despite having no connection with the parallel road of the same name that runs through Wailea and Mākena down below. For all the strictures of the rental companies – see p.170 – it takes appalling weather to render it unsafe, and in principle, for most of the year, it's possible to drive all the way along the south coast to Hāna, 37 miles away. However, as described on p.145, and as a result of the October 2006 earthquake that primarily affected the Big Island, the road was closed at the time this book went to press. If it remains closed, the fifty-mile round-trip to the point where you'd have to turn back, roughly 26 miles east of 'Ulupalakua, is not worth making. In case it has reopened by the time you read this, a detailed description of the route, coming in the opposite direction, begins on p.145.

Cafés

Café del Sol

3620 Baldwin Ave, Makawao
☏808/572-4877. Mon–Sat 8am–5pm,
Sun 8am–3pm. This daytime café
in Makawao's Courtyard Mall
serves espressos, pastries, salads,
sandwiches, and blue plate
specials, all for under $10, at
shaded garden tables.

Grandma's Coffee Store

Kula Hwy, Keōkea ☏808/878-2140.
While you're unlikely to see
"Grandma" herself at this
village café, there's plenty of
fresh Maui-grown coffee, plus
avocado sandwiches, salads,
macnut pesto, taro burgers,
and killer home-made cookies
or desserts such as blueberry
cobbler.

Restaurants

Café 808

Lower Kula Rd, Kula ☏808/878-6874.
Daily 6am–8pm. With just a few
plastic tables and chairs scattered
across a large bare floor, this
popular hangout, just above
the Holy Ghost Church, feels
much like a village hall, and
Upcountry residents gather here
all through the day. Breakfast
pancakes run $5, while later on
local favorites – "island grinds"
like *loco moco*, *saimin*, teriyaki
beef, or chicken katsu – cost
well under $10.

Casanova's

1188 Makawao Ave, Makawao
☏808/572-0220, ⓦwww
.casanovamaui.com. Mon & Tues
5.30am–12.30am, Wed–Sun
5.30am–1am. The 1970s Art
Nouveau–style lettering and
faded exterior of this single-
story wooden building in the
heart of Makawao belies its
status as one of Maui's hottest
nightspots. There's a dance floor
and bar just inside the door,
a romantic Italian restaurant
stretches further back, and
the breakfast deli/espresso
bar is alongside. Lunchtime
salads, pastas, and sandwiches
range from $6–16, while in
the evening, wood-fired pizzas
cost $12–20, pasta entrees are
$12–18, and specials are $22–28.
Portions are huge. The $5 cover
charge on dance nights (unless
you dine) can rise to $10 when
there's live music (typically Fri
and Sat).

Hali'imaile General Store

900 Hali'imaile Rd, Hali'imaile
☏808/572-2666. Mon–Fri 11am–
2.30pm & 5.30–9.30pm, Sat & Sun
5.30–9.30pm. One of Maui's very
best restaurants, serving gourmet
Hawaiian food in a large, bright
and smart former store in the
village of Hali'imaile, which
is two miles down Baldwin
Avenue from Makawao and
then a mile west towards

▼ CASANOVA'S

▲ HALI'IMAILE GENERAL STORE

Haleakalā Highway. Appetizers (up to $20) include an Asian pear and duck taco, and fresh island fish cakes; entrees, like Szechuan barbecued salmon or rack of lamb Hunan style, can cost over $30; and there's also a raw bar. Lunch is served on weekdays only.

Kitada's Saimin

3617 Baldwin Ave, Makawao ☎808/572-7241. Mon–Sat 6am–1.30pm. Very old-fashioned local-style diner, open from dawn until lunchtime only. A huge bowl of *saimin* can be had for $5, while burgers, sandwiches, and plate lunches cost little more.

Kula Lodge

Haleakalā Hwy, Kula ☎808/878-1535, ⊛www.kulalodge.com. Daily 6.30am–9pm. The wood-furnished dining room of *Kula Lodge* is open until the evening, but it's busiest at the start of the day, when most of the customers are already on their way back *down* Haleakalā. The food is American, with a definite Pacific Rim tinge; the lunch menu consists of sandwiches, burgers, and a few selections from the dinner menu ($11–18), while evening offerings include a *miso* oysters Rockefeller appetizer ($16), and lamb osso buco or *lilikoi* prawns (upwards of $30). Protea blossoms adorn the tables, and the views are immense.

Kula Sandalwoods

15427 Haleakalā Hwy, Kula ☎808/878-3523. Mon–Sat 6.30am–2pm, Sun 6.30am–noon. Homegrown upcountry produce forms the basis of the menu at this attractive little restaurant, on the *mauka* (mountain) side of the highway just before Haleakalā Crater Road heads off towards the summit. Open for breakfast and lunch only, with waffles and omelets earlier on replaced by $8–13 lunch specials including soup and sandwiches.

Makawao Sushi & Deli

3647 Baldwin Ave, Makawao ☎808/573-9044. Mon–Thurs 11.30am–3pm & 5–9pm, Fri & Sat 11.30am–3pm & 5–10pm, Sun 3.30–9pm. This smart little place on the main drag started out as a coffee bar, and still serves panini, espressos, and smoothies, but these days it's better known for its good, inexpensive sushi, with individual rolls from $3, eight-piece specialty rolls at $15–18, and sashimi plates from $17. Good-value lunches include a chef's bento box for $8.

Polli's

1202 Makawao Ave, Makawao ☎808/572-7808. Mon–Sat 7am–10pm, Sun 8am–10pm. Busy, good-value Mexican restaurant at Makawao's central crossroads, open for all meals daily. All the usual menu items are on offer, from chimichangas to fajitas (under $10), and they also do barbecue chicken and ribs on Mondays.

Haleakalā

Although the mighty volcano Haleakalā dominates Maui, it's hard to appreciate its full majesty until you climb right to the top. Hawaiian-style shield volcanoes are much less dramatically steep than the classic cones of popular imagination, and with its summit often obscured by clouds, Haleakalā can seem no more than a gentle incline. Around a million people each year make the journey, with many timing their climb to the top to coincide with the dawn, when the sun rises above the far side of the crater – but don't imagine that it's not worth coming later in the day. Winding Haleakalā Highway provides the only route, ascending more than ten thousand feet above sea level in a mere 38 miles. Beyond the verdant upcountry, it leads through purple-blossoming jacaranda, firs, and eucalyptus to reach open ranching land, then sweeps in huge curves to awe-inspiring Haleakalā Crater itself. Almost eight miles across, this eerie wasteland would comfortably hold Manhattan. It makes a superb spectacle at any time of day, but best of all is mid-afternoon, when the sun lights up its staggering array of russet cinder cones, ashen slopes, pockmarked craters, and craggy cliffs. It's also possible to hike into the crater, and even to spend the night there.

The summit drive

From all the major accommodation centers on Maui, the quickest route to the top of Haleakalā is to head for Kahului, and then follow Haleakalā Highway into the Upcountry. Also known from there on as Haleakalā Crater Road, it continues all the way to the summit, entering the park after a twisting twelve-mile climb through meadows, and reaching the park headquarters shortly after that and ending at the summit a further ten miles on.

Assuming you join the majority in attempting to drive up to Haleakalā Crater to witness the sunrise (around 5.50am in midsummer and 6.50am in midwinter) – and don't feel that you have to, as the views can be wonderful at any time of day – you'll need to make a very early start and a long hard drive in the dark. Allow two full hours to get to the top from Lahaina, Kā'anapali, or Kīhei, or one and a half hours from Kahului or Wailuku. If you end up late for the sunrise, be warned that you'll be driving straight into the dazzling sun, and watch out for the endless posses of downhill bikers coming the other way.

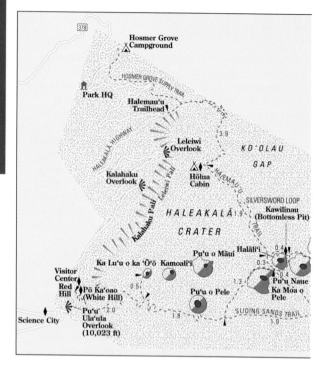

Before setting out, keep in mind that the last gas station before the summit is at Pukalani, 28 miles below; the last food and lodging is at *Kula Lodge* (see p.114), 22 miles short.

▼ HOSMER GROVE

Hosmer Grove and Waikamoi Preserve

Just beyond the park entrance a short road off to the left leads to the park's main campground, at Hosmer Grove. Set almost exactly at the mountain's tree line, this may look like a pleasant wooded copse, but in fact it marks the failure of an early-twentieth-century experiment to assess Maui's suitability for timber farming. Out of almost a hundred different tree species planted by Ralph Hosmer, only twenty survived, though that's enough to provide a nice thirty-minute nature trail.

By way of contrast, Waikamoi Preserve, adjoining Hosmer Grove, is a five-thousand-acre tract of upland rainforest that's

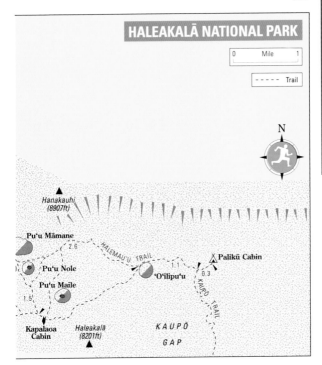

Hanakauhi (8907ft)

Pu'u Māmane

2.6

HALEMAU'U TRAIL

X Palikū Cabin

1.1

'O'ilipu'u

0.3

KAUPŌ TRAIL

Pu'u Nole

Pu'u Maile

1.5

Kapalaoa Cabin

Haleakalā (8201ft)

KAUPŌ GAP

home to a wide assortment of indigenous Hawaiian birds. You can only hike through it with an authorized guide, so call ahead to see when the next of the Park Service's regular free Waikamoi Cloud Forest Hikes is scheduled (see box, p.119 for contact details).

It's possible to walk all the way into Haleakalā Crater from Hosmer Grove; a supply trail up the mountain meets the Halemau'u Trail after 2.5 miles, just short of the crater rim.

Halemau'u Trailhead

Haleakalā Crater Road, 2.5 miles up from the park headquarters.

Three approaches, each marked by a parking lot, lead into the crater beyond the park headquarters. The first of these, the Halemau'u Trailhead, signals the start of one of the park's two main hiking trails – described in detail on pp.120–124 – but there's nothing to see at the parking lot. The edge of the *pali*, where the trail actually drops into the crater, is almost a mile away.

Leleiwi Overlook

4.5 miles from the park headquarters.

Set a couple of hundred yards beyond its parking lot, Leleiwi Overlook offers views across the isthmus to West Maui, as well as a first glimpse into Haleakalā Crater, but you'll probably have seen enough of West Maui from the Crater Road, and better vantage points over the crater lie ahead.

▲ LELEIWI OVERLOOK

Kalahaku Overlook

It's only legal to stop at the Kalahaku or "Silversword" Overlook, a couple of miles short of the visitor center, as you drive *down* rather than up the mountain; in fact it's easy to pass by without noticing it at all. That's a shame, because this sheltered viewpoint provides perhaps the best overall prospect of Haleakalā Crater. Mauna Kea on the Big Island is often visible through the Kaupō Gap in the ridge to the right, and when the clouds clear you can also see down to the north coast of Maui. Unless you hike into the crater, this may be the only place you see any silverswords; in theory, there should be a few in the small enclosure below the parking lot, across from the overlook.

Haleakalā Visitor Center

Eleven miles from the park entrance. Summer daily 6am–3pm, winter daily 6.30am–3pm; no phone. Although the highway continues beyond it, most visitors consider they've reached the top of Haleakalā when they pull in at the Visitor Center. The railed open-air viewing area beside the parking lot commands great views of Haleakalā Crater. In the pre-dawn chill, however, many people prefer to admire the procession of red-brown cinder cones, marching across the moonscape far below, through the panoramic windows of the small visitor center itself. If you're feeling more energetic, follow the short paved trail to the right instead, which leads up Pa Ka'oao, or White Hill, for 360° views.

The exhibits inside the visitor center are pretty minimal, though there's a good 3-D model of Haleakalā to help you get oriented. Park rangers also provide hiking tips and lead free guided-hikes, such as the Cinder Desert walk, which sets off from here along the Sliding Sands Trail (see p.120) and the Waikamoi Cloud Forest Hike from Hosmer Grove. Call the park headquarters for current schedules (see opposite).

Haleakalā National Park practicalities

Entrance and fees

Haleakalā National Park remains open around the clock; $5 per pedestrian or cyclist, $10 per vehicle, valid for three days in both sections of the park; $25 for Tri-Parks Annual Pass, which also covers Hawaii Volcanoes National Park, and Pu'uhonua O Hōnaunau National Historic Park on the Big Island; national passes are sold here and valid for admission.

The park headquarters

The park headquarters looks out across central Maui from alongside the highway, three quarters of a mile up from the park entrance (daily 8am–4pm; ☎808/572-4400 information, ☎808/871-5054 weather; ⊛www.nps.gov/hale). This is the place to enquire about the day's quota of camping places, or to register if you've managed to reserve a cabin. It holds little by way of exhibits or printed information, but you can pick up a basic park brochure and buy detailed hiking maps.

Camping in the park

Hosmer Grove is the only Haleakalā campground accessible by car, and the only one for which campers do not need to obtain permits. Fifty sites, in a soft sloping meadow surrounded by tall pines, are available free on a first-come, first-served basis, with a three-night maximum stay.

Backcountry camping, in the sense of simply pitching your tent in some remote spot, is not permitted anywhere in the park. There are, however, three rudimentary, but sound, backcountry cabins within Haleakalā Crater, which can only be reached on foot. All are on the grassy fringes of the crater, sheltered by the high surrounding cliffs, and are padlocked to deter casual backpackers from wandering in. Each is rented to one group only per night, and has twelve bunk beds, with no bedding, plus a kitchen, a stove for heating, and an outhouse. Hōlua and Palikū cabins offer tent camping in the adjacent meadows – the 25 daily permits are issued on a first-come, first-served basis at the park headquarters, between 8am and 3pm daily – but Kapalaoa Cabin does not. Water is normally available, but it's up to you to purify it before you drink it.

Permits to stay in the cabins are heavily oversubscribed, and limited to three days in total, with no more than two days at any one cabin. In a system that prioritizes island residents, you have to apply in writing at least three months in advance, stating the exact dates you want, to Haleakalā National Park, PO Box 369, Makawao, HI 96768 (contact ☎808/572-4400 or ⊛www.nps.gov /archive /hale/pages/tier_two/cabins.htm for more information). A lottery at the start of each month decides the schedule for the month ahead; successful applicants are requested to pay $75 per cabin per night. To check on possible cancellations, call ☎808/572-4459 between 1pm and 3pm daily.

Outfitters

Companies that offer "downhill biking" trips down Haleakalā, and horse-riding expeditions in the crater, are listed on p.178

Pu'u Ula'ula (Red Hill)

A few hundred yards up the highway from the visitor center. A smaller parking lot at a final loop in the road stands just below Pu'u Ula'ula, or Red Hill – at 10,023 feet, the highest spot on Maui. A circular shelter at the top of a short stairway offers what feel like aerial views of Haleakalā

▲ PU'U ULA'ULA (RED HILL)

Confusingly, the peak that officially bears the name of Haleakalā is five miles east, above Kapalaoa Cabin, and a couple of thousand feet lower.

Science City

The road beyond Pu'u Ula'ula is closed to the public, but leads in a few more yards to the gleaming white domes of Kolekole or Science City. This multinational astronomic research facility, perched at the top of the House of the Sun, monitors the earth's distance from the moon by bouncing laser signals off a prism left there by the Apollo astronauts.

The Sliding Sands Trail

Beginning at the visitor center parking lot, the very demanding Sliding Sands Trail briefly parallels the road to skirt White Hill. It then starts its leisurely switchback sweep into the crater, down a long scree

Crater. In clear conditions – soon after dawn is the best bet – you may be able to see not only the 80 miles to Mauna Loa on the Big Island, but even the 130 miles to Oahu.

The geology of Haleakalā

Dramatic, multicolored Haleakalā Crater, 10,023 feet above sea level at the summit of Haleakalā, and measuring more than seven miles long, two miles wide and half-a-mile deep, is often hailed as the largest extinct volcanic crater in the world. As far as geologists are concerned, however, it's none of these things. Not only is the "crater" not a crater at all – in shape, size, origin and location it bears no relation to any summit crater Haleakalā may once have possessed – but strictly speaking it's not even volcanic, having been created by erosion rather than eruption.

Fueled by the same "hot spot" that has created all the volcanoes of Hawaii, Haleakalā originally thrust its way from the ocean around 800,000 years ago. In the 400,000 years that followed, it first fused with, and eventually came to dominate, the West Maui Mountains. At its highest, it may have stood 15,000 feet tall, which is higher than Mauna Kea and Mauna Loa on the Big Island today.

The volcano then slumbered for several hundred thousand years, during which time torrential rainfall eroded away its topmost 6000 feet, and sculpted vast canyons into its flanks. Two of these valleys, Keanae to the north and Kaupō to the east, cut so deeply into the mountain that they met in the middle, creating a huge central depression. When the "hot spot" beneath Haleakalā finally reawakened, a series of smaller eruptions poured another 3000 feet of lava into that cavity, and gushed out of the Ko'olau and Kaupō gaps to refill the valleys. Peppering the summit with raw red cones of cindery ash, it made it look to the untrained eye like the sort of crater you might expect to find at the top of a volcano.

▲ SILVERSWORDS ON SLIDING SANDS TRAIL

slope of soft red ash. While the *pali* to the north of the visitor center is scattered with buttresses of rock and patches of green vegetation, this side is almost completely barren, the smooth crumbling hillside only interrupted by an occasional bush. Far ahead, mists and clouds stream into the crater through the Koʻolau Gap.

It takes a while to appreciate the immensity of the crater; for the first mile, you expect to arrive at the crater floor at a group of multicolored rocks in the middle distance, but when you reach them you find a longer descent ahead.

Two miles down, the trail passes between a clump of twenty-foot-high ʻaʻā rock outcroppings. A spur trail from here leads 0.4 miles, by way of a miniature "garden" of silverswords, to the smooth lip of the Ka Luʻu O Ka ʻŌʻō Crater. This full round cinder cone, glinting with pink, red, yellow, and ochre highlights in the bright sun, cradles a hollow core filled with tumbled boulders. From the trail above,

you can see long clinker flows extending for two miles north of it, eating away at the neighboring Kamaoliʻi Crater.

Continuing on the main trail, you wind down through a rough field of ʻaʻā lava. In season, the silverswords that almost line the path shoot up above head height. For the final stretch of the total 3.8-mile descent, the desolate crater floor spreads out broad and flat ahead of you, punctuated by heaped mounds of ash.

You'll know you've reached the crater floor when you strike the south end of the clearly marked spur trail that connects the two main trails. Turning left towards the Halemauʻu Trail involves a fairly stiff climb across the flanks of the ruddy Ka Moa O Pele cinder cone; over to the right, the triangular mountain peak of Hanakauhi can be seen rising beyond Puʻu Naue.

The Halemauʻu Trail

The alternative route down into the crater, the switchbacking Halemauʻu Trail, starts at a

Hiking In The Crater

The only way to get a real sense of the beauty and diversity of Haleakalā Crater is by hiking down into it. Although there are just two principal trails – the Sliding Sands and Halemau'u trails – the terrain varies far more than you could ever tell from the crater-edge viewpoints, ranging from forbidding desert to lush mountain meadows.

The obvious problem is that, once you've descended into the crater, you'll have to climb back out again, which at an altitude of 10,000 feet is never less than grueling. That said, reasonably fit hikers should be able to manage a day-hike that takes them down one trail and back up the other – a minimum distance of eleven miles, which is likely to take at least seven hours. More ambitiously, you could aim to take in Kapalaoa Cabin along the way, for a total of thirteen miles and more like eight hours, but heading any further east would be unrealistic. The easier route is to go down Sliding Sands and back on Halemau'u, though since the trailheads are several miles apart, you'll need to arrange a pickup or hitch a ride between the two. A parking lot near the Halemau'u Trailhead (see p.117) makes the ideal spot for hitchhikers hoping to get a lift back up the mountain.

If you've arranged to stay overnight in the crater, you could see the whole thing in two days, although most hikers spend longer. It takes a hardy and very well-prepared backpacker, however, to trek out via the Kaupō Trail to the south.

Don't underestimate the effects of the altitude. Allow an hour or so in the summit area to acclimatize before you set off on the trails; not only will that prepare you for the effort ahead, but it will also mean that you're still close to the road if you start to feel ill. By far the most effective treatment for altitude sickness is to descend a few thousand feet. Scuba divers should not go up Haleakalā within twenty-four hours of a dive; ask your dive operator for detailed advice.

You should also be prepared for the cold. Temperatures at the summit at dawn are likely to be around freezing, while rain clouds are liable to drift into the crater at any time of the day, and seriously chill anyone without warm waterproof clothing.

Finally, Haleakalā is such an ecologically delicate area that it's essential to practice minimum impact hiking. Carry out everything you carry in, take all the water you need (reckon on six pints a person a day), and stick to established trails. Above all, never walk on the cinder soil surrounding a silversword plant.

trailhead half a dozen miles down Haleakalā Crater Road from the visitor center. Towards the end of the relatively featureless 0.75-mile descent from the parking lot to the crater rim, the main trail is joined by a side trail up from Hosmer Grove. Eventually the trail crosses a high, narrow ridge; provided the afternoon clouds aren't passing over it, you'll get staggering views down to the north Maui coastline, as well as south into the crater.

Only the first few switchbacks cross back and forth between the north and south sides of the high bluff. Here at the tip of the Leleiwi Pali, it's very obvious how the landscape below has simply poured down through the Ko'olau Gap, from the crater towards the ocean. Soon, however, the trail narrows to drop sharply down the south side of the *pali*; it never feels too dangerous, though the drop-offs are enormous. The tiny shape of the overnight Hōlua Cabin comes into view a couple of miles ahead, a speck at the foot of the mighty cliff.

The trail eventually levels out beyond a gate at the bottom of the final switchback, then undulates its way through a meadow filled with misshapen and overgrown spatter cones towards Hōlua Cabin, just under four miles from the trailhead. A slight detour is required to reach the cabin itself, where the lawns are often filled with honking *nēnē* geese. Beyond it, the trail climbs on to a much more rugged *a'a* lava flow, the youngest in the crater area. Indentations in the rocky outcrops are scattered with red-berried *'ōhelo* bushes, nurtured by the wet clouds that drift in through the Ko'olau Gap.

As you climb slowly towards the heart of Haleakalā Crater, you can branch away to the left to follow the brief Silversword Loop, which holds the park's greatest concentration of silversword plants.

The crater floor

At the point where the Halemau'u Trail reaches the crater floor, almost six miles from its start, a bench enables weary hikers to catch their breath while contemplating the onward haul around the north side of the Halāli'i cinder cone. If you continue south, and turn right after 0.3 miles, you'll come to the foot of the Sliding Sands Trail 1.3 miles after that.

Keep going to the left, however, and within a couple of hundred yards the Halemau'u Trail follows the crest of a low ridge to make a serpentine twist between Halāli'i and the nameless cinder cone to the north. Known as Pele's Paint Pot, this gorgeous stretch is the most spectacular part of Haleakalā Crater, the trail standing out as a lurid red streak of sand against the brown and yellow mounds to either side. You can tell that Halāli'i is of relatively recent origin by the fact that its rim has not yet worn smooth; look back to see the park visitor center framed far away on the crater rim.

It's possible to loop right around Halali'i and head back along either trail, but the Halemau'u Trail continues east for another four miles. Immediately north of the junction where you're forced to decide, you'll see the fenced-off hole of Kawilinau, also known,

▼ THE HALEMAU'U TRAIL

Silverswords

Haleakalā is a treasure trove of unique flora and fauna, but the most distinctive of species of all is the silversword. A distant relative of the sunflower, presumably descended from a lone seed that wafted across the Pacific from America, this extraordinary plant has adapted perfectly to the forbidding conditions of Haleakalā Crater.

Known by the ancient Hawaiians as the 'āhinahina, or "silvery-gray," it consists of a gourd-shaped bowl of curving gray leaves, a couple of feet across, and cupped to collect what little moisture is available. Slender roots burrow in all directions just below the surface of the low-quality cinder soil; merely walking nearby can crush the roots and kill the plant.

Each silversword takes between three and twenty years to grow to full size, and then blossoms only once. Between May and June of the crucial year, a central shaft rises like a rocket from the desiccated silver leaves, reaching a height of three to eight feet, and erupting with hundreds of reddish-purple flowers. These peak in July and August, releasing their precious cargo of seeds, and the entire plant then withers and dies.

misleadingly, as the Bottomless Pit; in fact, this small volcanic vent is just 65 feet deep. Spatters of bright-red rock cling to its edges, but it's not especially remarkable. Ancient Hawaiians are said to have thrown the bones of important chiefs into it, to ensure their remains would never be disturbed. Half a mile further east, you have the additional option of cutting south across the crater, between Pu'u Naue and Pu'u Nole, to meet the Sliding Sands Trail near Kapalaoa Cabin.

The hike to Kapalaoa Cabin

If you continue east rather than heading left where the Sliding Sands Trail meets the crater floor – which you'll only have time to do if you're camping down in the crater – you enter a landscape that resembles the high mountain valleys of the western United States. The trail runs at the foot of a steep *pali*, on the edge of a delightful alpine meadow carpeted with yellow flowers, including the primitive native *moa*. Two miles along, shortly after two successive turnoffs to the left – one is an official

trail, one a "trail of use," but it's impossible to tell which is which, and in any case they soon join to cut across to the Halemau'u Trail – you come to Kapalaoa Cabin. This small, wood-frame, green-roofed cabin, on a slight mound tucked beneath the peak that's officially named Haleakalā, is the only overnight shelter in the crater that doesn't have its own campground; for details of how to make a reservation, see box on p.119.

Palikū Cabin

East of Kapalaoa, the Sliding Sands Trail has two more miles to run before it finally merges with the Halemau'u Trail at the 'O'ilipu'u cinder cone, and the two then run together a further 1.4 miles to Palikū Cabin. The hike all the way here from the crater rim and back up again is too far to attempt in a single day; only press on if you've arranged to stay overnight. The last three miles along either trail involve a gentle descent through sparsely vegetated terrain that turns progressively greener as you approach Palikū. There are actually two cabins at Palikū, one for public use and one for the rangers; both are nestled beneath a sheer cliff, where an attractive, but generally dry, meadow gives way to a well-watered strip of forest.

Kaupō Trail

The very demanding, nine-mile Kaupō Trail heads south from Palikū Cabin, first through the Kaupō Gap to the edge of the park, and beyond that all the way down to meet the Pi'ilani Highway on Maui's remote south coast. It takes a couple of miles to escape the pervasive cindery dryness of the crater flow, but once past it you find you've crossed to the rain-drenched eastern side of the island.

As the walls of the Kaupō Gap rise to either side, the trail drops through dense forest, then, once out of the park, descends steeply through lush grazing land. Now that you're on Kaupō Ranch land, be scrupulous about staying on the correct trail; free-ranging bulls roam on the other side of many of the fences. After several hours of extravagant switchbacks, you finally reach the highway 200 yards east of the Kaupō Store (see p.146). Unless you've arranged to be picked up, your problems may just be beginning – little traffic passes this way. If Pi'ilani Highway is still closed, as it was at the time this book went to press (see p.145), the only safe way to make the hike would be to leave a vehicle of your own parked at the Kaupō Store, having driven it there via Upcountry Maui.

Some people make the entire hike from the summit to Kaupō in a single day, on the basis that doing so means that they don't have to reserve a cabin or campsite or carry a heavy pack. That's an exceedingly long and demanding day-hike of just over eighteen miles, however, and not one you should attempt without prior experience of hiking in Haleakalā.

▲ PELE'S PAINT POT

The road to Hāna

Sculpted by rainwater cascading down the northern slopes of Haleakalā, Maui's northeast coast holds the island's most inspiring scenery. From Kahului, the Hāna Highway winds for fifty miles through this spectacular landscape to the time-forgotten hamlet of Hāna, twisting in and out of gorges, past waterfalls and over more than fifty tiny one-lane bridges. All year, but especially in June, the route is ablaze with color from orchids, eucalyptus, and orange-blossomed tulip trees, while little fruit stands and flower stalls make tempting places to stop. This memorable drive is almost always done as a day-trip. While not as hair-raising as popular legend would have it, the driving is slow going, taking around three hours each way. If you'd rather keep your eyes on the scenery than on the road, take a tour.

Ho'okipa Beach County Park

Two miles east of Pā'ia. The best windsurfing site in Maui, if not the world, is Ho'okipa Beach County Park. Thanks to a submerged rocky ledge that starts just a few feet out, the waves here are stupendous, and so are the skills required to survive in them – this is no place for beginners. The peak season for windsurfing is summer, when the trade winds are at their most consistent.

By longstanding arrangement, sailboarders can only take to the water after 11am each day. In the early morning, and on those rare winter days when the wind dies down, expert surfers flock to Ho'okipa to ride the break known as "Pavilions" near the headland to the east.

As a beach, Ho'okipa is not hugely attractive. It's unshaded for most of its length, apart from a nice big grove of trees at the western end. Picnic shelters,

▲ HO'OKIPA BEACH COUNTY PARK

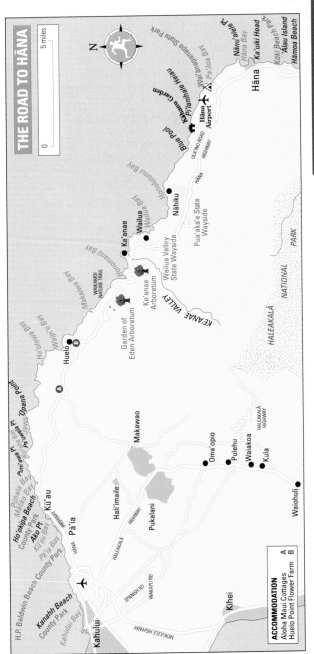

showers, and restrooms are ranged along a platform of lava boulders raised above the small shelf of sand. In summer, the surf can be low enough for swimming, but you still have to negotiate the seaweed-covered ledge to reach deep enough water.

Ho'okipa is so busy that you can only approach it along a one-way loop road, which starts beyond its far eastern end; the auxiliary parking lot on the headland here is a great place from which to watch or photograph the surf action.

Huelo

Although the coastal road around East Maui is called Hāna Highway from the moment it leaves Kahului, it changes from Hwy-36 to Hwy-360 ten miles east of Pā'ia, at the foot of Hwy-365 from Makawao, and that's where you'll find mile marker 0.

The first potential distraction as you head towards Hāna is the unsigned turnoff, marked by a double row of mailboxes at a bend in the highway roughly 3.5 miles along, that leads down to the village of Huelo. The dirt road soon passes the plain Kaulanapueo ("resting-place of the owl") Church, built of coral cement on a black lava base and usually kept locked. It continues for a couple of miles, but neither it nor its many side roads offer access to the sea. Like many local communities, Huelo has become an uncertain mixture of Hawaiians and wealthy *haoles*.

Not far beyond the road down to Huelo, the picnic table immediately below the Huelo Lookout fruit stand offers an opportunity to stop and admire the views of the forested slopes and the ocean beyond.

Waikamoi Nature Trail

Just over half a mile beyond the mile 9 marker. The one place where you can explore the forested ridges above the Hāna Highway is along the enjoyable Waikamoi Nature Trail which sets off from an obvious roadside pull-out. This one-mile loop trail starts beyond a small picnic shelter, gently zigzagging up a muddy ridge. Despite the stone benches along the way, there are no views to speak of – it's barely possible to see beyond the tight-packed *hala* trees and green rustling bamboos hemming the track – but sunlight dapples down through the overhead canopy to magical effect. Here and there, you pass a variety of eucalyptus trees whose bark peels like fine tissue paper. The trail tops out at a smooth grassy

Jaws

Thanks to mouthwatering photo spreads in many a surfing magazine, Maui's most famous surf site these days is Jaws, a highly inaccessible spot further on beyond Ho'okipa where 70-foot waves have occasionally been recorded. Surfing there has only become at all practicable since the advent of tow-in surfing, using jet skis, in the early 1990s, and Hawaii's premier surfers now flock here in winter to do battle with monsters that typically measure around 50ft. If you want to watch the action, you can reach Jaws by turning left towards the ocean five miles east of Ho'okipa, between mileposts 13 and 14 on Hwy-36; follow Hanaha Road until your vehicle can take no more, which will probably be soon in an ordinary rental, then hike oceanwards between the pineapple fields.

▲ WAIKAMOI NATURE TRAIL

clearing, with another picnic shelter, and a large mosquito population. It makes little difference whether you return by the same route, or down the adjacent jeep road that drops directly to the parking lot.

A little further along the highway, Waikamoi Falls tumbles down towards the road at a tight hairpin bend. If you want a closer look, the only place to park is immediately before the bridge – a spot that is all too easy to overshoot.

Garden of Eden Arboretum

Hwy-360, not far beyond Waikamoi Falls ☎ 808/572-9899, ⓦ www .mauigardenofeden.com. Daily 8am–3pm. $10. The small and privately owned Garden of Eden Arboretum displays an attractive assortment of colorful flowers and orchids. It also offers a slightly distant waterfall view, and has picnic tables with a panoramic prospect of the coastline.

Honomanū Bay

Shortly after mile marker 13, the highway drops back down to sea level for the first time since Ho'okipa Beach, and you finally start to get the long coastal views for which it's famous. The Ke'anae Peninsula appears on the horizon, but much closer

at hand – where the gorgeous, uninhabited Honomanū Valley, lit up by tulip trees, gives way to the ocean – you'll see the black gravel beach at Honomanū Bay. Swimming and snorkeling here is only advisable on the calmest of summer days, but it's a popular site with local surfers.

Two separate dirt tracks cut down to the shore from the road as it sweeps around the narrow valley. The first, at 13.5 miles, leads down to the north shore of the stream; the second, just after the 14-mile marker on the far side of the stream, is paved for the first few yards, but then becomes steeper and muddier. It comes out at the longer side of the beach.

Ke'anae Arboretum

Hwy-360, Ke'anae. Daily dawn–dusk. Free. From a wooded bend in the road a few hundred yards before the 17-mile marker, a paved, level trail heads inland to the attractive public gardens of the Ke'anae Arboretum. Following the course of a stream you can hear but not see, it leads into a lush, narrow valley and reaches the arboretum within a quarter of a mile.

Fifty-foot-high clumps of "male bamboo" guard the entrance, with tropical plants

▲ KEʻANAE ARBORETUM

Keʻanae Peninsula

Not far beyond the arboretum, a side road twists down to the flat Keʻanae Peninsula, the site of a small, and still predominantly Hawaiian, village. It's said that this windswept promontory consisted of bare rock until a local chief forced his followers to spend two years carrying baskets of soil down the mountainside; thereafter it became a prime *taro*-growing region, and supported a large population.

The *taro* fields are still here, surrounded by abundant banana trees and birds of paradise, and there's also a fine old church among the tall palms. The edge of the ocean is as bleak as ever, with *hala* trees propped up along the shoreline and the surf crashing onto headlands of gnarled black lava; swimming here is out of the question.

A small pavilion nearby holds the best public restrooms on the whole route to Hāna.

beyond including Hawaiian species such as torch ginger and wet and dry *taro*. Beyond the *taro* fields, a mile into the park, the trail becomes a wet scramble through the rainforest, crossing up and over the valley ridge by way of tree-root footholds. Along with lots of small waterfalls, and swarms of tiny flies feasting on fallen guava and breadfruit, there's a good chance of spotting rare forest birds and even wild boar.

Wailua

Within a mile of Keʻanae, as the highway veers inland, the arrow-straight Wailua Road plunges down to another

▲ KEʻANAE PENINSULA

traditional village, Wailua. Unlike Ke'anae, its ancient rival, Wailua has always been fertile and still holds extensive *taro* terraces.

The lower of the two churches that stand a short way down from the turnoff is known as the Coral Miracle. Local legend has it that, in 1860, just as its builders were despairing of finding the stone to complete it, a freak storm washed up exactly enough coral on the beach below. It's a simple but attractive chapel, painted white, with turquoise stenciling around the porch and windows. Look back across the valley as you leave the building for a superb view of the high Waikani Falls, garlanded by flowering trees at the head of the valley.

Wailua Road ends just above the tranquil mouth of Wailua Stream, which makes a sharp contrast with the ocean pummeling the beach of black pebbles beyond. Don't drive down to the stream – there's no room to turn round – and don't even consider a swim.

Wailua Valley State Wayside

Lookouts to either side of the highway beyond the Wailua turnoff offer scenic views up and down the coastline. From the inconspicuous *mauka* parking lot of Wailua Valley State Wayside, steps climb through a tunnel of trees to a vantage point overlooking Wailua Valley as it reaches the sea, and also inland across Ke'anae Valley, to towering waterfalls, undulating ridges, and endless trees.

Wailua Lookout

Just past the mile 19 marker.
Beneath the Wailua Lookout, the thickly wooded gorge of Wailua Valley spreads like a little oasis, with the taller of Wailua's

two churches, St Gabriel's, poking its head above the sea of trees. At the next bend, just around the corner, a big cascade roars beside the road; you have to react quickly to stop.

Pua'aka'a State Wayside

22.5 miles along Hāna Highway. The spacious parking lot of Pua'aka'a State Wayside is every bit as big as the park itself. In fact, this is a favorite stop for bus tours, because so little effort is required to negotiate the park's few yards of paved trails. If you brave the crowds, you'll see a pretty sequence of small waterfalls, with picnic tables dotted on either side of a stream.

Nāhiku

Not far after the mile 25 marker, a narrow unmarked road takes about three miles to wind down to the ocean. The few houses along the way constitute Nāhiku, though there's no town, just a jungle of trees and vines, some of which all but engulf the

PLACES The road to Hāna

▲ NĀHIKU

abandoned vehicles left here. The road comes out at Ōpūhano Point, from where you can look back towards Wailua atop the tree-covered cliffs reaching down into the water.

Early in the twentieth century, Nāhiku was the site of the first, albeit unsuccessful, rubber plantation in the US. Subsequently, ex-Beatle George Harrison had a home here, but in his later years he only visited occasionally, following a bitter legal dispute with his neighbors that centered on the construction of a beach-access footpath.

Just before the mile 29 marker, it's well worth stopping at the cluster of roadside shacks, centered on the *Nāhiku Fruit Stand*, which sell souvenirs, drinks, and snacks.

Kahanu Garden

'Ula'ino Road, Hāna ☏ 808/248-8912 or 332-7234, ⊛ www.ntbg.org. Mon–Fri 10am–2pm. $10, under-13s free.

The first sign that you're finally approaching Hāna is when you pass Hāna Gardenland, a not very exciting commercial nursery, on the right.

Immediately afterwards, 'Ula'ino Road drops away to the left of Hwy-360. Three quarters of a mile down, just after the road crosses a minor ford, you'll find the entrance to Kahanu Garden, a nonprofit facility belonging to the National Tropical Botanical Garden. Over a hundred acres are devoted to tropical plants, but the land is most significant as the site of Pi'ilanihale Heiau, the largest ancient *heiau* (temple) not merely in Hawaii but quite possibly in the entire Pacific. A *luakini*, or temple where human sacrifice took place, its original construction has been

dated to the late thirteenth century, but it's thought to have been enlarged and re-dedicated by Pi'ilani around 1570 AD to celebrate his then-recent conquest of the entire island. It was rebuilt once more in the late eighteenth century, and extensively restored and reconstructed during the 1990s.

A mile-long loop trail through Kahanu Garden begins by skirting the edge of an extensive forest of splay-footed *hala* trees. A free booklet describes the traditional uses of several different species of indigenous and imported plants that have been cultivated along the way.

Your first sight of the *heiau* itself presents it towering above the lush oceanfront lawns. Constructed from black lava boulders, intricately slotted into place, and set on a natural lava flow, it's an impressive spectacle. Measuring 174 metres by 89 metres, it covers almost three acres and consists of five separate tiers on its oceanward side. As usual at such sites, however, in deference to ongoing Hawaiian religious beliefs, visitors are not allowed to set foot on the actual structure and can only admire it from a distance. As a result, you're not likely to spend more time here than the half-hour it takes to walk the trail, which also offers some gorgeous views along the coast.

The Blue Pool

'Ula'ino Road continues beyond Kahanu Garden as a rougher but still mostly paved track, almost always negotiable with care in an ordinary rental car as it undulates gently through the woods for another 1.4 miles. There are no long-range views, but it's a lovely

▲ THE BLUE POOL

stretch of countryside. The road ends abruptly in a shady grove a hundred yards short of the ocean, just above a stream whose outlet is blocked by a natural wall of heavy black boulders.

In recent years, the existence of a fabulous waterfall a short walk from here, popularly known as the Blue Pool, has become common knowledge among visitors to Maui. The area has therefore become rather too popular for its own good, and local residents have been infuriated by the sheer quantity of day-trippers who find their way down here. Some have succumbed to the inevitable by turning their gardens into parking lots, while others have confronted visitors and refused to let them through. If you do come this way, it's currently impossible to predict what your reception will be.

Assuming the situation has been resolved by the time you read this, don't expect to park for free right at the bottom of the road, but keep going in any case as far as you can — prices get cheaper further down, so you can expect to pay around $2 rather than the $4 on offer higher up.

To reach the shimmering Blue Pool itself, make for the shoreline, then head left for a hundred yards. Less than twenty yards from the sea, the pool is constantly replenished by water cascading from the *hala*-covered ridge above. It's set in a grotto that's festooned with ferns, vines, and *hala* trees, its mossy walls bursting with tiny pinks and peonies. As you sit on the rocks, fresh water from the falls splashes your face, while you can feel the salt spray of the ocean on your back. It's also possible to walk to the right along the beach, where coconuts lie among the boulders. Atop a spit of rough *'a'ā* lava, five minutes along, you can watch the surf crashing and grinding the black rocks to hollow out little coves, while a jungle of *hala* trees lies, unreachable, beyond.

Wai'ānapanapa State Park

Within two miles of Hāna, beyond the turnoff to Hāna Airport, a clearly signed road *makai* (oceanwards) from the highway leads through a "tunnel" of overhanging trees to the shoreline at Wai'ānapanapa State Park. To reach the main parking lot, perched above a tiny black-sand beach, turn left when you reach the park cabins at the end of the first straight stretch of road. A short and easy trail descends from the parking lot to this beautiful little cove, where the beach changes from shiny black pebbles to fine black sand as it shelves into the ocean. It looks wonderful, and barely has room to hold its daily crowd of sunbathers, but swimming is deadly, with heavy surf and deep water just a few yards out.

At the right-hand side of the beach as you face the sea, look for a hollow cave in the small cliff that you just walked down. Squeeze your way through its narrow entrance and you'll find that not only does it widen inside, it is, in fact, a tunnel. The far end, where it's open to the ocean, is a truly magical spot.

By contrast, a very short loop trail to the left of the parking lot back at the top leads down and through Waiʻānapanapa Cave. A few yards back from the sea, this "cave" is actually a collapsed lava tube, holding two successive grotto-like pools. It's slightly stagnant and smells rather like a public restroom, but you do see some nice clinging flowers.

Coastal hiking trails in both directions make it easy to escape the throngs at the beach. Heading northwest (left), you're soon clambering over a headland of black lava through a forest of *hala* and *naupaka*. Inlets in the jagged shoreline harbor turquoise pools, while the surf rages against the rocks; in places, where the sea has hollowed out caverns, you can feel the thud of the ocean beneath you. A painting of a natural "lava bridge" here,

executed in 1939 by Georgia O'Keeffe, now hangs in the Honolulu Academy of Arts. A mile or so along, the trail ends at the fence of Hāna Airport.

Southeast of the beach, the footpath crosses smoother, firmer lava, passing the park campground, a cemetery, and an impressive blowhole. After around a mile, it reaches the ruined Ohala Heiau, the walls of which remain clear despite ivy-like *naupaka* growing inside. You can continue four miles on to Hāna; the scenery is invigorating all the way, but the trail gets progressively harder to follow.

Waiʻānapanapa is by far the nicest place on Maui to camp beside the ocean (see p.166).

Hāna

For some visitors, the former sugar town of Hāna comes as a disappointment after the splendors of the Hāna Highway. There's no question that the point of driving the road is to enjoy the scenery en route, rather than to race to Hāna itself. Still, it's a pleasant enough little place, and remains one of the most relaxing spots on Maui to spend a few days; short

▲ WAIʻĀNAPANAPA STATE PARK

▲ HĀNA

on swimmable beaches and golf, perhaps, but very long indeed on character, history, and beauty.

Although in ancient times Hāna controlled a densely populated region, these days it's home to just a few hundred inhabitants. Having long resisted any concept of "development" for its own sake, they proudly see themselves as one of the most staunchly traditional communities in the state.

When the local sugar plantation closed in 1943, most of its land was bought by Paul Fagan, a Californian businessman. He established not only the Hāna Ranch, whose cowboys still work cattle herds in the fields above town, but also modern Maui's first hotel,

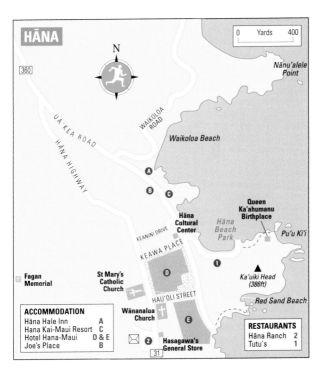

▲ SUNSET OVER HĀNA

the *Hotel Hāna-Maui*. Fagan died in 1959 – he's commemorated by a large white cross on the hillside – but the town remains dominated by the businesses he founded. Most of the town's central area is taken up by the *Hotel Hāna-Maui*, while the Hāna Ranch headquarters on the main highway houses its most conspicuous restaurant and other utilities.

Downtown Hāna

None of the buildings along the main highway, which passes through Hāna a hundred yards up from the ocean, is especially worth exploring, though Wananalua Church, whose square, solid tower contrasts appealingly with the flamboyant gardens surrounding it, makes a photogenic landmark. Across the road, the Hāna Ranch Center is a dull little mall, designed to feed and water the daily influx of bus tours, but given a flash of color by the odd *paniolo* cowboy. The original Hasegawa's General Store, stocked with every item imaginable, burned down in 1990. Now located in a charmless former theater, it's still a friendly place to pick up supplies.

Hāna Cultural Center

Uaʻkea Road, Hāna ☎808/248-8622. Daily 10am–4pm. $2 suggested donation. Local history is recalled by the low-key exhibits – gourds, calabashes, fishhooks, and crude stone idols – at the Hāna Cultural Center, down from the highway and above the bay. It also holds art exhibitions and is amassing a comprehensive collection of photos of past and present Hāna residents. A tiny nineteenth-century jail-cum-courthouse shares the same driveway, while a replica living compound has been constructed in the grounds alongside, of the kind used by the ancient Hawaiian *makaʻainana* (common people). As well as a thatched stone dwelling and a canoe house, it features garden terraces planted with *taro* and *ti*.

Hāna Bay

Broad Hāna Bay is much the safest place to swim in East Maui, as well as being the only protected harbor in the area. The small gray-sand beach known as Hāna Beach County Park spreads to the south, at the foot of Keawa Place, backed by lawns that hold picnic tables, restrooms, and changing rooms. The park's long terraced pavilion, pressed against the curving hillside across the road, houses *Tutu's* takeout counter (see p.139).

Thrusting into the ocean further south, the high cinder cone of Kaʻuiki Head is the bay's most prominent feature. Now covered with trees, it used to be just a bare rock, and served as a fortress for the ancient chiefs of Maui; Kahekili is said to have repelled an invasion from the Big Island here in 1780. Its far side – only seen easily from the air – collapsed into the sea long ago.

A short hiking trail – hard to spot at first, but soon clear enough – heads off around Ka'uiki Head from beyond the jetty, offering excellent views across the bay and up to Hāna itself. Soon after a tiny red-sand beach, it reaches a bronze plaque, set into a slab of rock near a couple of small caves in the base of the hill. This marks the birthplace of the great Hawaiian queen, Ka'ahumanu, though she was probably born

later than the year it says, 1768. Continuing on, you discover that the rocky point beyond is in fact an island. Known as Pu'u Ki'i, it was once topped by a giant *ki'i* (wooden idol), erected by the Big Island chief, Umi; an automated lighthouse now stands in its place. Around the next corner, the trail is blocked by an impassable red scree slope.

Red Sand Beach

A precarious coastal footpath leads along the south flank of Ka'uiki Head to a lovely little cove that shelters one of Maui's prettiest beaches, Red Sand Beach. The Hāna Ranch, which owns the land here, considers the walk so dangerous that it makes every effort to discourage visitors; the path is often closed due to serious erosion,

Queen Ka'ahumanu: scenes from a life

No figure encapsulates the paradoxes of early Hawaiian history as completely as Queen Ka'ahumanu, the daughter of Nāmāhana, a chiefess from East Maui, and Ke'eaumoku from the Big Island. Her parents' strategic alliance presented such a threat to Kahekili, the ruling chief of Maui, that they were fleeing for their lives when Ka'ahumanu was born at Hāna, around 1777.

Chief Ke'eaumoku was one of Kamehameha the Great's closest lieutenants. His daughter may have been as young as eight when she first caught the eye of the king; soon afterwards, she became the seventeenth of his twenty-two wives.

Ka'ahumanu was Kamehameha's favorite wife. As a high-ranking *ali'i*, she possessed great spiritual power, or *mana*. She was also an expert surfer and serial adulterer. It was after Kamehameha's death, in 1819, that she came into her own. Announcing to her son Liholiho that "we two shall rule over the land," she proclaimed herself Kuhina Nui, or Regent, and set about destroying the system of *kapus*. This elaborate system of rules denied women access to certain foods and, more importantly, to the real source of power in ancient Hawaii – the *luakini* war temples. At first Ka'ahumanu's goal was to break the grip of the priesthood, but in 1825 she converted to Christianity, after being nursed through a serious illness by Sybil Gingham, the wife of Hawaii's first missionary. Meanwhile, in 1821, she had married both the last king of Kauai, Kaumuali'i, and his seven-foot-tall son, Keali'iahonui.

Ka'ahumanu outlived Liholiho, who died in England in 1824, and remained the effective ruler of Hawaii when his younger brother Kauikeaouli succeeded to the throne. After seven years spent proselytizing for her new faith, she died on June 5, 1832. Her last words were reported as "Lo, here am I, O Jesus, Grant me thy gracious smile."

▲ RED SAND BEACH

and should only be attempted after seeking local advice as to current conditions. To find it, walk left from the south end of Ua'kea Road, below a small, neat Japanese cemetery. Approximately a five-minute walk, the path follows, and in places spans, a narrow ledge around a hillside of loose red gravel, but at this low elevation it's not too nerve-racking.

Behind a final promontory, the beach lies angled towards the rising sun, shielded by a row of black dragon's-teeth rocks, kept well flossed by the waves. Hawaiians know this canoe landing as Kaihalulu Beach. It's only ever safe for swimming in the tiny inshore area, and even then the razor-sharp rocks beneath the surface make it essential to wear reef shoes. The origin of the beach's coarse reddish cinders – the eroded red cliffs above it – is very obvious, and it's equally obvious that you can hike no further.

Shops

Hāna Coast Gallery

Hotel Hāna-Maui, Hāna ☎808/248-8636. Probably the best array of Hawaiian arts and crafts on the island, including sculptures, turned wooden bowls and furniture, ceramics and featherwork, and plenty of paintings of East Maui landscapes.

Restaurants

Hāna Ranch

Hāna Hwy, Hāna ☎808/248-8255. Restaurant Sun–Tues & Thurs 8–10am & 11am–3pm; Wed, Fri & Sat 8–10am, 11am–3pm & 6–8.30pm; takeout daily 6.30am–4pm. Unenthralling quick-fire restaurant in the heart of Hāna, specializing in bland lunches for the daily hordes of bargain-seeking day-trippers. Mostly it's fries with everything, but a half-pound burger made from local beef costs $12.50, and they do a vegetarian *taro* burger too. Dinner is served on Wednesday, Friday and Saturday only, and is slightly more interesting; $18–35 entrees, such as barbecue ribs or teriyaki chicken, include a salad bar. A cheaper takeout counter sells *saimin* for $3.50 and plate lunches for around $8.

Ka'uiki

Hotel Hāna-Maui, Hāna Hwy, Hāna ☎808/248-8211. Daily 7.30–10.30am, 11.30am–2.30pm & 6–9pm. The deluxe resort's open-sided, wicker-furnished dining room ranks among the most expensive restaurants in

Hawaii, which can make its downhome ambience and local-style service seem a little odd. Thanks to recent improvements in the kitchen, however, the food is truly superb. A real commitment to using local ingredients and techniques results in magnificent fish dishes in particular, such as *hapu* (sea bass) steamed with coconut in *ti* leaves as an entree, or a *ceviche* appetizer of *onaga* (red snapper). A changing three-course dinner menu costs $60; lunch is much simpler, centering on classy burgers and sandwiches for around $18, while breakfast is a relaxed delight.

Nāhiku Fruit Stand

Just before the 29-mile marker on Hwy-360, Nāhiku. No phone. This funky, friendly roadside shack sells delicious espressos and smoothies, along with homemade lunches such as banana bread and fish specials.

Pauwela Café

375 W Kuiaha Rd, Ha'ikū ☎808/575-9242. Mon 7am–2.30pm, Tues–Fri 7am–2.30pm & 5–8pm, Sun 8am–2pm. Occupying one corner of the rusting gray hulk of Pauwela Cannery, a mile off Hwy-36 and roughly five miles east of Pā'ia, this cheerful, classy neighborhood café serves delicious, inexpensive breakfasts – try the *pain perdu* (French toast) – plus salads, sandwiches, and lunch specials, all priced close to $6.

Tutu's

Hāna Bay, Hāna ☎808/248-8244. Beachfront takeout counter, whose indifferent sandwiches, burgers, plate lunches, sodas, and lemonades attract long queues every lunchtime.

Up In Smoke BBQ

Just before the mile 29 marker on Hwy-360, Nāhiku. No phone. The perfect lunchtime snack if you're driving the Hāna Highway; a simple open-air grill that serves superb $6 kebabs or tacos of smoked or fresh-caught fish, and also baked breadfruit.

Entertainment

Paniolo Lounge

Hotel Hāna-Maui, Hāna Hwy, Hāna ☎808/248-8211. This relaxed, friendly bar provides the only nightlife option in the whole of East Maui. While it serves the cocktails and snacks you might expect, the real reason to come is to enjoy the performances of traditional and contemporary Hawaiian music by local musicians, which take place Thursday through Sunday evenings. Don't expect a late night; it's all over by 9.30pm.

▼ HĀNA RANCH RESTAURANT

Beyond Hāna

Even if you only have a single day to explore East Maui, it's well worth continuing beyond Hāna. For its first few verdant miles, the scenery along Pi'ilani Highway is even more gorgeous than what came before. While the most obvious destination for day-trippers is the waterfall-strewn 'Ohe'o Gulch, some great beaches lie just south of Hāna. Until recently, anyone averse to returning the way they came could choose in normal weather to follow Pi'ilani Highway right around the whole barren coastline of southern Maui and into the Upcountry above Wailea. However, as detailed on p.145, Pi'ilani Highway was closed when this book went to press, so that journey had become impossible. Enquire locally to find out whether the isolated, partially unpaved road has reopened.

Kōkī Beach Park

A couple of miles south of Hāna, the Haneo'o Loop Road heads left from the highway. After half a mile, it reaches the ocean alongside the white sands of Kōkī Beach Park. Local surfers and boogie-boarders love this spot, but unless you're a very confident swimmer and all-round watersports expert, take heed of the many signs that warn of a very dangerous rip-current just offshore. It's a great place for a coastal stroll, in any case.

The exposed red cinder cone that dominates Kōkī Beach is named Ka Iwi O Pele, or "the bones of Pele", as the volcano goddess was supposedly killed here by her sister, the goddess of the sea. Oprah Winfrey, who has purchased a number of lots in the vicinity from the Hāna Ranch, has built a home on a

▲ KŌKĪ BEACH PARK

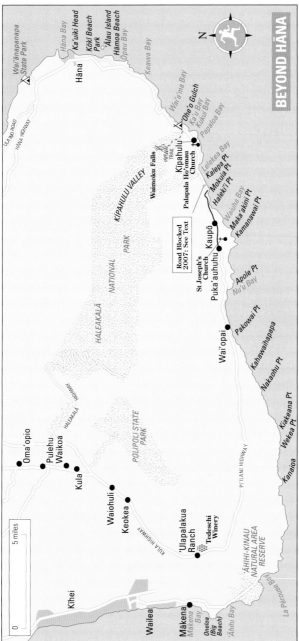

hundred-acre plot immediately north.

Just south of Kōkī Beach, tiny Ā'lau Islet stands just out to sea. Ancient Hawaiians reshaped the lava rocks along the promontory closest to the island to create artificial fishponds, and fishermen are still frequent visitors.

Hāmoa Bay

1.5 miles down Haneo'o Loop Road. A couple of small roadside parking bays allow access to the grey-sand beach at Hāmoa Bay, used by *Hotel Hāna-Maui* for all its oceanfront activities, including a weekly *lū'au*. Once the site of a small settlement destroyed by the tsunami of 1946, it's a good surfing spot, and holds a nice picnic area as well, but it's unsafe for swimming.

The highway continues south from Hāmoa Bay through a succession of tiny residential villages, where, apart from the odd roadside fruit stand and countless crystal-clear waterfalls, there's no reason to stop.

'Ohe'o Gulch

10 miles south of Hāna. At beautiful 'Ohe'o Gulch a natural rock staircase of waterfalls descends to the

▲ 'OHE'O GULCH

oceanfront meadows at the mouth of the Kīpahulu Valley. This far-flung outpost of Haleakalā National Park (see p.115), sometimes spuriously known as "Seven Sacred Pools," tends to be jam-packed in the middle of the day, but, as one of the few places on Maui to offer easy access to unspoiled Hawaiian rainforest, it shouldn't be missed. If you hike a mile or two into the hills, you'll soon escape the crowds to reach

'Ohe'o Gulch practicalities

The national park at 'Ohe'o Gulch remains open 24 hours per day, and charges its standard admission fee of $10 per vehicle to all users of the roadside parking lot. That covers access to the entire park for three days, so unless you manage to visit 'Ohe'o Gulch and the summit crater (see p.115) within two days of each other, you'll have to pay twice. A ranger station just down the slope from the lot has up-to-date information on local roads and hiking trails (daily 9am–5pm; ☎808/248-7375). Guided hikes to different destinations set off daily except Saturdays at 9.30am; for details of trips on horseback in the vicinity, see p.179. Access to the upper reaches of the Kīpahulu Valley, regarded as one of the most pristine and environmentally significant regions in all Hawaii, is barred to the public. The park is, however, hoping to purchase large tracts in the valleys to the west, in order to open more hiking trails and remote beaches.

For details on camping at 'Ohe'o Gulch, see p.166.

cool rock pools, which so long as it's not raining are ideal for swimming.

Kūloa Point Trail

The paved footpath that leads downhill from the 'Ohe'o Gulch parking lot – officially, Kūloa Point Trail – is so busy that it's forced to operate as a one-way loop. Get here early if you want to enjoy it before the onslaught, but don't avoid it otherwise. After ambling through the meadows for five minutes, the trail winds past ancient stone walls on the low oceanfront bluff, and then down to a tiny gray-grit beach, where the shark-infested ocean is far from tempting.

However, upwards from the ocean, a "ladder" of stream-fed pools climbs the craggy rocks, an ascent negotiated by suckerfish in breeding season. Several of the pools are deep and sheltered enough for swimming, and on calm sunny days the whole place throngs with bathers. It's impossible to follow the stream as far up as the high road bridge; by that point, the gorge is a slippery, narrow water chute.

Pīpīwai Trail

The Pīpīwai Trail, into the mountains above 'Ohe'o Gulch, ranks as one of the very best hikes in Hawaii (though one on which it's essential to carry mosquito repellent). Occasionally it's closed by bad weather, but the construction of two sturdy footbridges has ensured that the first mile or so is almost always accessible. It starts beside the ranger station, but swiftly crosses the highway and heads uphill through steep fields, where thick woods line the course of the 'Ohe'o Stream.

After the first half-mile, which is by far the most demanding stretch of the hike, you come to a railed overlook facing the towering 200-foot Makahiku Falls. A little further up, a deep groove in the earth heads right, leading to a series of shallow bathing pools just above the lip of the falls, where the stream emerges from a tunnel in the rock. As well as commanding magnificent views, it's an utterly idyllic spot for a swim on rain-free days.

Continuing along the main trail, you immediately pass through a gate in a fence, to emerge into an open guava orchard where you'll soon hear the thundering of smaller waterfalls to your right. There's no way to get to the water, but you'll see it framed through the thick jungle, together with the gaping cave mouth it has hollowed out on the far side. A little further on, you may be lured off the trail again by

▼ PĪPĪWAI TRAIL

a pair of twin falls near a small concrete dam, which can be admired from a rocky outcrop in the streambed below.

Beyond that lies a lovely meadow, with views to the high valley walls in the distance, laced by huge waterfalls. A mile up, the trail crosses high above the stream over the bridges and then follows a dark and narrow gap through a forest of huge, old bamboo interspersed with sections of level wooden boardwalk. Eventually, two miles up from the road, you'll spot the spindle-thin, 400-foot Waimoku Falls ahead. Reaching its base requires a lot of scrambling, and close to the end you have to cross the stream itself on stepping stones. Despite the obvious danger of falling rocks, many hikers choose to cool off by standing directly beneath the cascade. Allow a good two hours to complete the entire round-trip hike.

Kīpahulu

Within a mile of ʻOheʻo Gulch, the highway passes through the village of Kīpahulu. Time seems to have stood still in this attractive little spot since the local sugar mill closed down eighty years ago. The only sign of life these days comes from the occasional lunchtime fruit stand selling mangoes, papayas and the like, fresh from the roadside orchards.

Palapala Hoʻomau Church

A quarter-mile beyond milepost 41 at Kīpahulu, a paved road branches left off the highway. After a couple of hundred yards, turn left again onto a dirt road through a "tunnel" of trees, and park by the giant banyan tree at the end that guards the Palapala Hoʻomau Church. Founded in 1864, it has whitewashed coral walls and a green timber roof, and is set in pretty clifftop gardens. The interior is utterly plain and unadorned.

Visitors make their way to this tranquil spot because the fenced-off platform of black lava stones in the churchyard holds the grave of Charles Lindbergh

▼ PALAPALA HOʻOMAU CHURCH

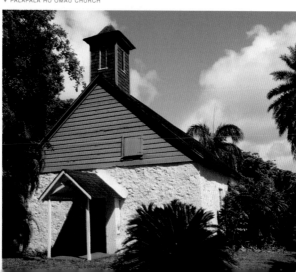

▲ KĪPAHULU POINT STATE PARK

(1902–74), who won fame in 1927 as the first man to fly across the Atlantic and later achieved notoriety as a Nazi sympathizer. Lindbergh retired to Maui late in life, and died within a couple of years.

Leading off from the cemetery, and only accessible through it, Kīpahulu Point Park is a small, shaded lawn, fringed with bright orange-leafed bushes, where the picnic tables command wonderful ocean views.

Along the South Maui coast: the Pi'ilani Highway

As described in the box alongside, Pi'ilani Highway was closed at the time of writing. If it has since reopened, expect to take roughly an hour and twenty minutes to drive along it from Kīpahulu to the Tedeschi Winery in Upcountry Maui, and a minimum of two hours to reach Kahului. Thus, it saves little if any time to return this way rather than back along the Hāna Highway. On the other hand, it will show you, literally, another side of the island, and one that still looks much as it did before outsiders ever reached Hawaii.

The countryside immediately beyond Kīpahulu is lovely, dotted with exclusive homes whose owners are no doubt happy that this is not yet a standard tourist loop. After less than two miles, Pi'ilani

Pi'ilani Highway Closure

When this book went to press, Pi'ilani Highway was still blocked as a result of an earthquake in October 2006. The problem was said to be that boulders had become perched in dangerous positions above the road itself. As the county authorities were not prepared to risk damage to vehicles down below, they had therefore comprehensively barricaded the Kukulula Bridge, near Kālepa Point, a couple of miles west of 'Ohe'o Gulch towards Kaupō. Enquire locally to find out whether it has reopened; even if it has, do not attempt to drive this route after dark.

Highway returns to sea level – for the first time in several miles – and skirts the long gray pebble beach at Lelekea Bay. As you climb the cliffs at the far end, look back to see water spouting out of the hillside above an overhang in the rock, forceful enough to be a gushing jet rather than a waterfall.

The pavement gives out after the second of the two little coves that follow. An overlook 2.3 juddering miles further on looks down on the small flat promontory holding the 1859 Huialoha Church. A mile after that, the solitary Kaupō Store is an atmospheric general store that's normally open on weekdays only.

By now, the landscape has become much drier, and you're starting to get views up to the Kaupō Gap, where a vast torrent of lava appears to have petrified as it poured over the smooth lip of Haleakalā Crater. To the east, you can peek into the lushness of the upper Kīpahulu Valley, but the slopes to the west are all but barren.

Beyond St Joseph's Church, which stands below the highway a mile beyond the Kaupō Store, the pavement starts up again and the road begins to mount the long southern flank of Haleakalā at the gentlest of angles. There's no tree cover on the deeply furrowed hillside, so cattle

Kahikinui

The southern shoreline of Maui used to be known as Kahikinui, or Tahiti Nui; the equivalent part of Tahiti, which has the same outline as Maui, bears the same name. Archeologists treasure it as one of the very few areas where Hawaii's modern population is so small that ancient habitation patterns and structures can still be readily discerned. They've dated several *heiaus* (temples) and other remains as having been constructed around the start of the seventeenth century, a time when it's thought Maui had just been united under a single ruler, Pi'ilani himself, for the first time.

gather beneath the occasional shade tree beside the road.

Naked russet cinder cones lie scattered to either side of the road, some bearing the traces of ancient Hawaiian stone walls, while rivers of rough black *a'a* lava snake down to the sea. An especially vast hollow cone, near the 20-mile marker, marks the spot where small huts and ranch buildings start to reappear. Soon Mākena becomes visible below, with Molokini and Lanai out to sea, and three miles on it's a relief to find yourself back in green woodlands. The Tedeschi Winery (see p.112) is a little over a mile further on, with another 23 miles to go before Kahului.

Lanai

The island of Lanai, nine miles west of Maui, measures just thirteen miles by eight. Thanks partly to its mysterious allure as a so-called "private island," it's a popular day-trip by ferry from Maui. Don't picture Lanai as the ultimate unspoiled Hawaiian island, however; it largely lacks the lush scenery and sandy beaches of its neighbors. Indeed, until the twentieth century, ancient Hawaiians and modern settlers alike barely bothered with this dry and barren mound of red dirt; then began its seventy-year reign as the world's largest pineapple producer. These days, Lanai belongs almost entirely to billionaire David Murdock, who has shut down the plantation and redeveloped Lanai as an exclusive resort. Almost all its three thousand inhabitants live in the former plantation village of Lāna'i City, 1600ft above sea level. This is also the site of all its hotels and restaurants, except for the *Mānele Bay Hotel*, on the south coast near Lanai's only swimming beach.

Mānele Bay

Ferries from Maui to Lanai arrive at Mānele Bay, on the south coast eight miles from Lāna'i City. As parched and barren as a Greek island, the bay is protected from the open ocean by the high flat-faced cliff on its eastern side, which glows red when it's hit by the setting sun. People fish from the rocks or picnic

Visiting Lanai

Scheduled flights serve tiny Lanai Airport, four miles southwest of Lāna'i City, from both Kahului on Maui and from Honolulu; see p.169.

For travelers based on Maui, however, the best way to reach Lanai is on the *Expeditions* ferry (☎808/661-3756 or 1-800/695-2624, ⓦwww.go-lanai.com; $25 each way, under-12s $20). It sails from Lahaina to Mānele Bay daily at 6.45am, 9.15am, 12.45pm, 3.15pm, and 5.45pm, while departures from Lanai are at 8am, 10.30am, 2pm, 4.30pm, and 6.45pm. The trip takes approximately 50 minutes, and the ferry operator intends to add extra sailings to Lanai from Mā'alaea on Maui's central isthmus in the near future.

The harbor is a very short walk from Hulupo'e Beach, the island's best, but shuttle buses also meet each arriving ferry at the harbor. They charge a $5 flat fare, whether you're going up to Lāna'i City or just taking the 500-yard hop to the *Mānele Bay Hotel*.

Many visitors also come to Lanai on day trips with Trilogy Ocean Sports (☎808/661-4743 ext 2387 or ☎1-888/225-6284, ⓦwww.sailtrilogy.com), whose Discover Lanai tour includes a barbecue picnic beside Hulopo'e Beach (adults $179, ages 3–15 $90).

▲ MĀNELE BAY

nearby, and the odd brave soul dodges the boats to go snorkeling, but there's nothing much here apart from an overpriced little snack bar, the *Harbor Cafe*.

Hulopo'e Beach

Only accessible by road from Mānele Bay, but also reached via a footpath down from the *Mānele Bay Hotel* (see p.166), curving, sandy Hulopo'e Beach

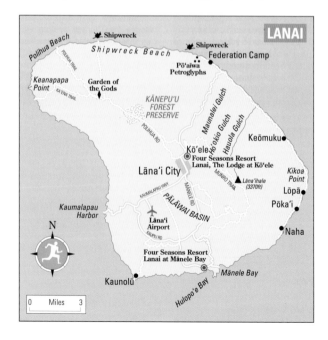

LANAI

Polihua Beach

Shipwreck

Shipwreck Beach

Shipwreck

Federation Camp

POHAKU TRAIL

Pō'aiwa Petroglyphs

Keanapapa Point

Garden of the Gods

KA ENA TRAIL

KĀNEPU'U FOREST PRESERVE

Maunalei Gulch

Ho'okio Gulch

Hauola Gulch

POLIHUA RD

Keōmuku

Kō'ele

Four Seasons Resort Lanai, The Lodge at Kō'ele

Lāna'i City

MUNRO TRAIL

Lāna'ihale (3370ft)

Kikoa Point

Lōpā

Pōka'i

KAUMALAPAU HWY

MĀNELE RD

PĀLĀWAI BASIN

Kaumalapau Harbor

Lāna'i Airport

KAUPILI RD

Naha

N

Four Seasons Resort Lanai at Mānele Bay

Kaunolū

Mānele Bay

Hulopo'e Bay

0 Miles 3

Exploring Lanai

Lanai has the most rudimentary road system imaginable, with less than thirty miles of paved highway, none of which runs along the coast. For visitors, the only significant stretches are the eight-mile Mānele Road from Lāna'i City down to Mānele Bay, and the four miles of Kaumalapau Highway between Lāna'i City and the airport. Free shuttle buses ferry guests at the three hotels along these routes; anyone who's using the restaurants, or simply looks confident, should have no problem hopping a ride.

There are two car rental outlets: Lāna'i City Service, based on Lāna'i Avenue in Lāna'i City (daily 7am–7pm; ☎ 808/565-7227 ext 23 or 1-800/JEEP-808), and the Adventure Lanai Ecocenter (☎ 808/565-7373, ⓦ www.adventurelanai.com), which doesn't have an office but will deliver a vehicle to anywhere you choose. There's no point in renting an ordinary car; the only way to explore the island is with a 4WD vehicle, along a network of rough-hewn, mud-and-sand jeep trails. Following heavy rain, many of those trails are closed to all traffic; don't rent a vehicle unless you're sure you can take it where you want to go.

A basic Wrangler Jeep costs around $140 per day, so most visitors cram all their sightseeing into a single 24-hour period. Both companies provide full instruction if you've never driven 4WD before, but neither offers any extra insurance; you're liable for any damage to your vehicle, which can easily amount to several thousand dollars for a basic mishap in the sand.

Lāna'i City Service also runs the island's only taxis (when there's a vehicle to spare), charging around $5 to the airport or Mānele Bay from Lāna'i City, and $10 from the airport to Mānele Bay.

In addition, Adventure Lanai Ecocenter offers guided jeep tours of the island, which involve some active hiking, at around $100 for a half-day trip. They also arrange half-day kayaking, quad-biking, and diving excursions; surfing lessons for kids; and rent out mountain bikes.

PLACES Lanai

is by far the best swimming beach on Lanai.

The only facility for hotel guests at the beach is a small equipment kiosk at the west end. Its main users tend to be local families rather than tourists, who come to swim, picnic, and explore the tide pools at the foot of Mānele Cone, the extinct cinder cone that divides Hulopo'e Bay from Mānele Bay. Both the tide pool area and the bays form a Marine Life Conservation Area. Spinner dolphins are regular visitors, and in the morning especially, the snorkeling here can be excellent. The offshore waters rank among the best diving sites in Hawaii. Regular dive trips are organized by Trilogy Ocean Sports

(☎ 808/565-7700 ext 2387 or ☎ 1-888/225-6284, ⓦ www .sailtrilogy.com).

The black lava walls of an ancient Hawaiian village are

▲ HULOPO'E BEACH

▲ THE PĀLĀWAI BASIN

The entire 15,000-acre basin – until just a few years ago, the largest pineapple field on earth – is a bowl-shaped depression. The high mountain ridge on its eastern side stands thousands of feet taller than the low rise to the west, while the bowl spills over altogether to flow down to the ocean on the southern side. Nothing is planted now in the fields, but the occasional vivid flowering tree lights up the highway.

clearly visible between the hotel and the beach. Sometimes it held permanent residents, who grew gourds and sweet potatoes, while during other periods it served as a seasonal fishing camp. Signs explain how the whole place used to look.

As detailed on p.166, it's possible to camp at Hulopo'e Beach.

The Pālāwai Basin

As you head up from the coast to Lāna'i City, it's easy to drive through the Pālāwai Basin, at the top of hill, without realizing that it's the collapsed caldera of the volcano that built Lanai.

Lāna'i City

To think of Lāna'i City as a town requires a stretch of the imagination; for it to call itself a "city" is little short of absurd. This neat, pretty community of just 2500 people was laid out on a basic grid in 1924 to house laborers from the plantations, and it has barely changed since. You have to search to find a two-story building: the leafy backstreets hold rows of simple cottages, identical but for the colors they're painted and the flowers in their gardens.

Virtually all the daily business of Lanai revolves around Dole Park. The main road, Lāna'i Avenue, runs along the park's

▼ LĀNA'I CITY

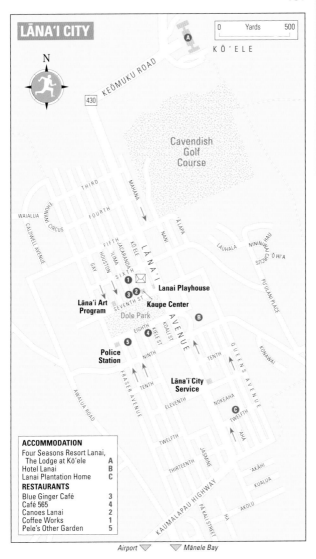

LĀNA'I CITY

KŌ'ELE

N

0   Yards   500

KEŌMUKU ROAD

430

Cavendish
Golf
Course

THIRD

MAHANA

'Ā'LAPA

WAIALUA

FOURTH

PŪNANA CIRCUS

CALDWELL AVENUE

NANI

LAUHALA

NININIWA CIRCUS

'Ō HI'A

PU'ULANI PLACE

FIFTH

JACARANDA

KŌ'ELE

'ILIMA

LĀNA'I

HOUSTON

SIXTH

GAY

❶

Lanai Playhouse

**Lānaʻi Art
Program**

❸ ❷

SEVENTH ST

Dole Park

Kaupe Center

KOALI ST

AVENUE

Ⓑ

❺

EIGHTH

❹

KELE ST

**Police
Station**

NINTH

QUEENS AVENUE

TENTH

KONAWAI

FRASER AVENUE

TENTH

**Lānaʻi City
Service**

NOKEAHA

AWALUA ROAD

ELEVENTH

TWELFTH

Ⓒ

TWELFTH

'AHA

'AKĀHI

THIRTEENTH

JASMINE

KUALUA

KAUMALAPAU HIGHWAY

PĀ KAI STREET

HA

'AKOLU

ACCOMMODATION
Four Seasons Resort Lanai,
  The Lodge at Kōʻele   A
Hotel Lanai   B
Lanai Plantation Home   C
RESTAURANTS
Blue Ginger Café   3
Café 565   4
Canoes Lanai   2
Coffee Works   1
Pele's Other Garden   5

Airport ▽   ▽ Mānele Bay

eastern end, while over a
hundred ninety-foot Cook
Island pines rise from the
wiry grassland in the center,
towering over the stores, cafés,
and offices that line all four
sides.

The Munro Trail

The only way to explore the
mountainous ridge that forms
Lanai's "backbone" is along
the ill-defined Munro Trail,
a twelve-mile loop trip from
Lānaʻi City that's much easier

to drive (in a 4WD vehicle) than it is to walk. This rutted track starts from the main road just north of *The Lodge at Kō'ele*, and climbs through a forest of towering Cook Island and Norfolk Island pines to the 3370-foot summit of Lāna'ihale. On clear days, that's the only spot in Hawaii from which it's possible to see five other islands.

Shipwreck Beach

On island maps, Keōmuku Road, which runs the full length of Lanai's east coast, might appear to offer plentiful beaches, sleepy long-lost towns, and ocean views. In reality it's a long, hard drive for very little reward, and you're better off simply driving its paved section as far as the sea, where drivers with 4WD vehicles can take a short detour north to Shipwreck Beach.

That name is informally applied to the whole of Lanai's northern shoreline, thanks to its remarkable history of maritime accidents. Countless vessels have come to grief in these shallow, treacherous waters; the coast is littered with fragments, while two large wrecks remain stuck fast a few hundred yards offshore. Some historians even believe that a sixteenth-century Spanish galleon was wrecked somewhere along here, long before Captain Cook reached Hawaii.

The sand road that leads to Shipwreck Beach peters out roughly 1.5 miles from the point where Keōmuku Road reaches the ocean. Walk in the same direction for a few yards, as far as a ruined lighthouse, to see the rusting orange hulk of a World War II "Liberty Ship" propped up on the rocks,

almost completely out of the water.

Walking two hundred yards inland from here brings you to a gulch where boulders still bear petroglyphs carved by ancient Hawaiians, including tiny stick drawings and bird-headed figures.

Garden of the Gods

Five miles northwest of Lāna'i City.
Lanai's most famous scenic spot is reached by a *very* dirty jeep drive across the thick, red dust bowl of the central plateau. The extraordinary Garden of the Gods looks more like the "badlands" of the Wild West than anything you'd expect to find in Hawaii. This small desert wilderness is predominantly a rich russet red, but its unearthly hillocks and boulders are scored through with layers of lithified sand of every conceivable hue – grays, yellows, ochres, browns, and even blues. At sunset, the whole place seems to glow, and the rocks lying scattered across the red sands cast long, eerie shadows.

During the 1980s, a trend spread across Hawaii in which locals erected rock cairns in isolated places in the belief that such "shrines" were an ancient Hawaiian tradition. Garden of the Gods was until recently filled with hundreds of cairns, but now that the practice is officially discouraged, and the old ones have toppled, it has reverted to something like its natural state.

Polihua Beach

Beyond the Garden of the Gods, fork right at the signpost to follow Polihua road, which drops steadily toward the ocean, cutting a groove into the red earth. It virtually never rains here – the clouds that drift over the plateau seldom reach this far – and the views are amazing.

At sea level, the road ends at the edge of broad Polihua Beach, where the red dust gives way to broad yellow sand. Over a hundred yards wide and 1.5 miles long, Polihua is a magnificent sight, and the chances are you'll have it to yourself. Until the 1950s, this remote spot was a favorite laying ground for green turtles – the name means "eggs in the bosom". They rarely turn up these days, but during the winter humpback whales can often be seen not far offshore, swimming in the Kalohi Channel. The current here is always too dangerous for swimming, though there's great windsurfing around the headland to the east. Beyond that stretches Kaiolohia or Shipwreck Beach; as described opposite, it's possible to hike its full eight-mile length.

Cafés

Café 565

408 Eighth St, Lāna'i City ☎808/565-6622. Mon–Fri 10am–3pm & 5–8pm, Sat 10am–3pm. As well as pizzas and calzones, this small café, with open-air seating alongside Dole Park, serves sandwiches, plate lunches, and even sushi.

Coffee Works

604 Ilima St, Lāna'i City ☎808/565-6962. Mon–Sat 6am–4pm. Spacious coffee bar a block north of Dole Park, behind the post office. Besides espressos, they also sell a few cheap sandwiches, smoothies, and ice cream, which you can enjoy on the large lāna'i.

Restaurants

Blue Ginger Café

409 Seventh St, Lāna'i City ☎808/565-6363. Daily 6am–8pm. Simple café-restaurant alongside Dole Park. It's a favorite local rendezvous, though the food is just basic plate lunches and pizzas, all for $7–10.

Canoes Lanai

419 Seventh St, Lāna'i City ☎808/565-6537. Daily 6.30am–1pm. A local-style diner, complete with swivel stools and soda fountain, serving burgers, *saimin*, and big fry-ups for breakfast and lunch only.

Formal Dining Room

The Lodge at Kō'ele, Lāna'i City ☎808/565-4580. Daily 6–9.30pm. Extremely formal restaurant, with a lofty reputation and silver-service treatment. Reserve early and savor the presentation as much as the food, which is a richer, meatier version of the usual upscale Hawaiian resort cuisine. Typical appetizers include *carpaccio* of venison and *foie gras*, both priced at around $20; entrees, upwards of $42, include rack of lamb, steak, and seafood; and there are some amazing chocolate desserts.

Hulopo'e Court

Mānele Bay Hotel, ☎808/565-7700. Daily 7–11am & 6–9.30pm. The less formal of the oceanfront hotel's two restaurants, the lovely, breezy *Hulopo'e Court* opens for breakfast and dinner only, charging $25 (full) or $17 (continental) for the morning buffet, and around $37 for delicious evening menu items such as steamed Hawaiian seafood *laulau*.

▲ HULOPO'E COURT

Lāna'i City Grille

Hotel Lanai, 828 Lāna'i Ave, Lāna'i City ☎808/565-7211. Wed–Sun 5–9pm. Friendly, intimate dining room, serving dinner only, but with an adjoining bar that remains open late each night. Now overseen by Maui chef Bev Gannon, owner of Maui's highly-rated *Hāli'imaile General Store* (see p.113), it serves an adventurous, largely organic menu of fresh local meat and seafood, accompanied by live music on Fridays.

Ihilani Dining Room

Manele Bay Hotel, ☎808/565-7700. Tues–Sat 6–9.30pm. The dinner-only *Ihilani Dining Room* serves "Mediterranean Gourmet" cuisine, with steamed and grilled island fish or roast meat for around $40.

Pele's Other Garden

Eighth Street and Houston, Lāna'i City ☎808/565-9628. Mon–Sat 10am–2.30pm & 5–8pm. Bustling health-food deli, with juices and wholesome $7 sandwiches to take out or eat in at lunchtime, which turns into a full-fledged Italian restaurant in the evening, with entrees like a gnocchi pasta special priced at $17–20.

The Terrace

The Lodge at Kō'ele, Lāna'i City ☎808/565-4580. Daily 6am–9.30pm. Marginally the less formal of *The Lodge's* two restaurants, with indoor and outdoor seating overlooking the lawns, serves health-conscious food, but still at quite high prices: even an egg-and-ham breakfast costs $14. Lunch is the best value, with $10 fresh-made soups and $15 grilled meat and fish dishes. Typical dinner entrees include slow-roasted lamb shank on couscous, and roasted chicken (both $30).

Accommodation

Accommodation

Maui is small enough to be easily explored from a single base; only if you'd like to spend time in the rainforests of East Maui is it worth booking rooms in two different places. Most of the island's accommodation options are concentrated close to its finest beaches in two highly developed coastal strips: on the lush leeward shoreline of West Maui, between Lahaina and Kapalua, or in what's known as South Maui, between Kīhei and Mākena on the drier and less scenic, but more central, southwest shoreline of the eastern half of the island. The most luxurious resorts of all are in Wailea in the south and Kā'anapali in the west, but there are cheaper alternatives nearby.

Travelers looking for a secluded paradise-island hideaway should consider the little B&Bs tucked away in Upcountry Maui and around Hāna. If you're not driving, Lahaina is the only place where you can stay in a real town with sightseeing, beaches, and restaurants within easy walking distance. For budget travelers, the cheapest options of all are in faded downtown Wailuku.

For a reliable selection of top-quality B&Bs, contact Hawaii's Best Bed & Breakfasts

(☎808/985-7488 or 1-800/262-9912, ⊛www.bestbnb.com), or Bed & Breakfast Hawaii (☎808/822-7771 or 1-800/733-1632, ⊛www.bandb-hawaii.com).

Lahaina

See the map on p.50 for locations of these listings.

Best Western Pioneer Inn 658 Wharf St ☎808/661-3636 or 1-800/457-5457, ⊛www.pioneerinnmaui.com. Maui's oldest hotel, on the seafront in the very center of Lahaina, makes a historic and highly atmospheric place to stay – though not as luxurious as the modern resorts – and often has last-minute availability. All the tastefully furnished rooms, which cost $165–185, have private baths and a/c, and open onto lovely *lānais*; the quieter ones face an inner courtyard, the rest overlook Banyan Tree Square. There's a small pool, but no on-site parking.

Lahaina Inn 127 Lahainaluna Rd ☎808/661-0577 or 1-800/669-3444, ⊛www.lahainainn.com. Set slightly back from Front Street above *David Paul's Lahaina Grill* (see p.57), this sumptuous, antique-furnished re-creation of how a century-old inn ought to look was actually built as a store in 1938. The twelve rooms of varying sizes have a/c, private bathrooms (most with showers rather than baths), and phones, but no TV. No children under 15 years. Rates range $145–195.

Lahaina Shores Beach Resort 475 Front St ☎808/661-3339 or 1-800/642-6284, ⊛www.lahainashores.com. Large, airy, shorefront hotel facing a pretty little beach a

---

While the average cost of a single night's accommodation is currently around $240 in high season, you can still expect to find a good hotel, condo, or B&B for more like $130. In theory, room rates are at their highest from Christmas to Easter, and from June to August – but don't expect to save more than perhaps $15–20 per night in a typical hotel by visiting in low season. Unless otherwise indicated, the room rates quoted throughout this chapter are for the cheapest double room in high season; all are subject to an additional state tax of 11.25 percent.

few hundred yards south of central Lahaina, next door to the 505 Front Street mall. Two-person rooms cost around $190, three- and four-person suites from $265; all have kitchens and *lānais*. An ocean view room costs around $30 more than a mountain view.

Old Lahaina House PO Box 10355 ☎808/667-4663 or 1-800/847-0761, ⊛www.oldlahaina.com. Good-quality B&B accommodation in a friendly private home with pool, a few hundred yards south of downtown Lahaina. There's one guest room in the house and four more in a separate garden wing; all are en-suite, with refrigerators, TVs, and a/c. Rates include breakfast on the *lānai*; rooms start at $69, suites at $119.

Outrigger Aina Nalu 660 Waineʻe St ☎808/667-9766 or 1-800/688-7444, ⊛www.outrigger.com. This sprawling but low-key condo complex, a couple of blocks from the sea in central Lahaina, has been through many incarnations over the years. Completely rebuilt and revamped in 2005, it now offers smart, well-equipped rooms in two X-shaped blocks, though with no beach and just a small pool, it's not a place to linger all day. Rack rates range from $209 for a studio up to two-bed, two-bath units from $319, but online deals can be much cheaper.

Plantation Inn 174 Lahainaluna Rd ☎808/667-9225 or 1-800/433-6815, ⊛www.theplantationinn.com. Luxury B&B hotel, close to the sea and styled after a Southern plantation home, complete with columns and verandahs and a twelve-foot-deep pool. All 19 rooms have bathrooms and *lānais*; prices start at $166, while the suites, which also have kitchenettes, cost $235–280. Guests get a discount at the downstairs restaurant, *Gerard's* (see p.58).

Kāʻanapali

See the map on p.62 for locations of these listings.

Hyatt Regency Maui 200 Nohea Kai Drive ☎808/661-1234 or 1-800/554-9288, ⊛www.maui.hyatt.com.

Condo rentals

Many of Maui's hotels double as condo properties, where individual owners also let out their apartments through various specialist agencies. In addition, these agencies often handle other privately owned vacation rentals, including ocean-front villas.

The agencies listed below offer a wide range of properties, generally at prices starting around $100 per night in low season, rising towards $150 between Christmas and March. Be sure to check whether there's an additional one-time "cleaning fee," which is usually around $50.

Kīhei

AA Oceanfront Condominium Rentals 1279 S Kīhei Rd, Kīhei ☎808/879-7288 or 1-800/488-6004, ⊛www.aaoceanfront.com

Condominium Rentals Hawaii 362 Huku Liʻi Place, #204, Kīhei ☎808/879-2778 or 1-800/367-5242, ⊛www.crhmaui.com

Kīhei Maui Vacations PO Box 1055, Kīhei, HI 96753 ☎808/879-7581 or 1-888/568-6284, ⊛www.kmvmaui.com

Maui Condominium and Home Realty 2511 S Kīhei Rd, Suite H, Kīhei ☎808/879-5445 or 1-800/822-4409, ⊛www.vacationweb.com/mchr

Māʻalaea

Māʻalaea Bay Rentals 280 Hauoli Street, Māʻalaea Village ☎808/244-7012 or 1-800/367-6084, ⊛www.maalaeabay.com.

Pāʻia

Maui Vacation Properties ☎808/575-9228 or 1-800/782-6105, ⊛www.maui.cc.

Kāʻanapali's grandest hotel, with opulent gardens, a palm-filled atrium with a pool of live penguins, and a vast labyrinth of swimming pools including a swinging rope bridge and bar. A ten-story main tower and subsidiary wings house more than eight-hundred luxurious rooms, four restaurants including the sumptuous *Sonʻz Maui at Swan Court* (see p.63), and a full-service oceanfront spa; a nightly *lūʻau* is held alongside (see p.64). Mountain-view rooms start at $365; expect to pay upwards of $450 for an ocean view.

Kāʻanapali Beach Hotel 2525 Kāʻanapali Parkway ☎808/661-0011 or 1-800/262-8450, ⊛www.kbhmaui.com. The least expensive option on Kāʻanapali Beach, located between Whalers Village and the Black Rock. This low-rise property, arrayed around attractive oceanfront lawns, has a fine stretch of beach plus a whale-shaped swimming pool complete with *tiki* bar. All of its large, well-equipped rooms have balconies or patios, though some offer a shower rather than bath. A strong commitment to preserving Hawaiian culture is reflected in regular classes and performances. Garden views from $205, ocean views from $265.

Outrigger Maui Eldorado 2661 Kekaʻa Drive ☎808/661-0021 or 1-888/339-8585, ⊛www.outrigger.com. Condo property consisting of several low buildings ranged up the hillside, well back from the shoreline; shuttle buses run to the resort's private beachfront area. All units offer a/c, *lānai*, maid service, washer/dryer, and a kitchenette or full kitchen. Rack rates start at $249, but typical online prices range from $179 to $309.

Royal Lahaina Resort 2780 Kekaʻa Drive ☎808/661-3611 or 1-800/280-8155, ⊛www.2maui.com. One of Kāʻanapali's two original resorts, commanding a long strip of perfect sand at the north end of the beach; it's been extensively upgraded during the last few years, but remains significantly cheaper than its neighbors provided you book online. While rack rates for its central 12-story tower of plush suites start at $410, you should be able to get a garden view

for half that, and an ocean view for under $300. They currently also offer a couple of dozen "cottages" of condo-style apartments on the grounds, though these may disappear in renovation, and any case they're not really worth the extra cost. Further amenities include two upscale restaurants, a nightly *lūʻau*, and a 3500-seat tennis stadium that's occasionally used for concerts.

Sheraton Maui Resort 2605 Kāʻanapali Parkway ☎808/661-0031 or 1-866/716-8109, ⊛www.sheraton-maui.com. This large luxury resort was the first to open at Kāʻanapali, in 1963, and has since been almost entirely rebuilt, with five tiers of rooms dropping down the crag of Black Rock and separate oceanfront wings, plus a lovely pool and lagoon, all at the broadest end of Kāʻanapali Beach. Garden-view rooms nominally start at $470, with ocean views from $555, though you may find limited discounts online.

The Westin Maui 2365 Kāʻanapali Parkway ☎808/667-25250031 or 1-866/716-8112, ⊛www.westinmaui.com. High-rise hotel in the center of Kāʻanapali Beach, immediately south of Whalers Village, where the five swimming pools are fed by artificial waterfalls and feature some great waterslides, and there's a lagoon of live flamingoes to match the predominantly pink decor. Not surprisingly, it's a major favorite for families with young children, so other guests can find it too noisy and hectic. Bright, modern, luxurious hotel rooms, all with private *lānai*, prices range upwards from $485 for a garden view, $570 for an ocean view.

The Whaler on Kāʻanapali Beach 2481 Kāʻanapali Parkway ☎808/661-4861 or 1-888/211-7710, ⊛www.the-whaler.com. Just north of Whalers Village, this condo resort holds comfortable one- and two-bedroom units, each with a lavish bathroom, *lānai*, and full kitchen. Most of the rooms don't face the ocean, and cost from $235 – those that do cost extra, starting at $280 – but all the accommodation itself is good, and there's also a small pool.

Northwest Maui

See the map on p.66 for locations of these listings.

Hale Maui 3711 Lower Honoapi'ilani Rd, Honokōwai ☏ 808/669-6312, ⊛ www.maui.net/~halemaui. Small family-run "apartment hotel" in Honokōwai, offering one-bedroom suites from just $95. They sleep up to five guests, with kitchens, washer-dryers, and *lānais*, but they have no phones, and there's limited maid service.

Kahana Reef 4471 Lower Honoapi'ilani Rd, Kahana ☏ 808/669-6491 or 1-800/451-5008, ⊛ www.mauicondo .com. Four-story row of well-furnished – if characterless – studios and one-bedroom units, right next to the sea, though there's little beach here. The rates are relatively low, starting at $155, but there's no a/c. Discounted car rental available.

Kahana Sunset 4909 Lower Honoapi'ilani Rd, Kahana ☏ 808/669-8011 or 1-800/669-1488, ⊛ www .kahanasunset.com. Luxury condos, spacious inside but squeezed close together, in lush gardens by a lovely sandy beach that's effectively restricted to guests only. Garden-view rates range $155; only the larger two-bedroom units, which cost from $235, enjoy ocean views.

Kahana Village 4531 Lower Honoapi'ilani Rd, Kahana ☏ 808/669-5111 or 1-800/824-3065, ⊛ www .kahanavillage.com. Large and very comfortable two- and three-bedroom condos, right beside the ocean if not a beach. The views are great, and the rooms good value for small groups, costing from $220 online, but the pool is small and the loft-like second bedrooms in the upper-level apartments can seem like an afterthought. Five-night minimum stay.

The Mauian 5441 Lower Honoapi'ilani Rd, Nāpili ☏ 808/669-6205 or 1-800/367-5034, ⊛ www.mauian.com. Very friendly, laid-back little resort, in vintage 1950s architectural style, facing ravishing Nāpili Beach and consisting of three two-story rows of tastefully furnished studio apartments with kitchenettes. Booked online, those nearest the ocean can start as low as $145; further back you'll pay around $20 less. The only phone and TV is in the communal lounge and library, which is also where the complimentary breakfast is served.

Nāpili Bay Resort 33 Hui Drive, Nāpili; reserve through Maui Beachfront Rentals, ☏ 808/661-3500 or 1-888/661-7200, ⊛ www.mauibeachfront.com. Small, fairly basic individually owned studio apartments for $145, in a superb oceanfront location on Nāpili Beach. Each has a kitchenette and *lānai*, and is capable of sleeping four guests.

Nāpili Kai Beach Resort 5900 Lower Honoapi'ilani Rd, Nāpili ☏ 808/669-6271 or 1-800/367-5030, ⊛ www.napilikai .com. While upgraded to the highest modern standards, this forty-year-old resort was built much closer to the ocean than would ever be allowed these days, so guests can enjoy breathtaking Nāpili Bay right on their doorstep. Rates aren't low, starting at around $250, but it's an independent property with a friendly old-time feel and a wonderful location; the *Sea House* restaurant is reviewed on p.70.

Noelani 4095 Lower Honoapi'ilani Rd, Kahana ☏ 808/669-8374 or 1-800/367-6030, ⊛ www.noelani-condo-resort.com. Fifty condo apartments of all sizes, set on a promontory, so all units enjoy views across to Molokai. Prices start at $125; amenities include cable TV and DVD, plus use of two oceanfront pools, a Jacuzzi, and laundry facilities.

Outrigger Royal Kahana 4365 Lower Honoapi'ilani Rd, Kahana ☏ 808/669-5911 or 1-800/447-7783, ⊛ www .outrigger.com. This oceanfront condo building, standing twelve stories high in central Kahana, enjoys views of Molokai and Lanai. While it's less intimate than the family resorts of Nāpili, it's undeniably smart, and all the a/c units, which include studios as well as one- and two-bedroom suites, have kitchens, washer-dryers, and private *lānais*. Garden view rooms start at $159, ocean views at $179.

ResortQuest Kā'anapali Shores 3445 Lower Honoapi'ilani Rd, Honokōwai ☏ 808/667-2211 or ☏ 1-877/997-6667, ⊛ www.kaanapalishores.com. Grand oceanfront condo development, right on the beach at the south end of Honokōwai, with two nice pools and a/c throughout. Booked online, typical rooms, which are on the small side, start at $179, while the large family suites are good value, costing from $205. Tennis is free, but parking costs $9 per night.

ResortQuest at Papakea Resort 3543 **Lower Honoapi'ilani Rd, Honokōwai** ☎808/669-4848 or ☎1-877/997-6667, ⓦwww.resortquesthawaii.com. Oceanfront Honokōwai complex of condo suites of all sizes, priced from $197 for the smallest. They're housed in eleven buildings arranged around two matching gardens, each of which has a pool, spa, lagoon, and putting course.

Ritz-Carlton, Kapalua 1 **Ritz-Carlton Drive, Kapalua** ☎808/669-6200 or 1-800/241-3333, ⓦwww.ritzcarlton .com. The sheer elegance of this opulent, marble-fitted *Ritz-Carlton* can make it feel a bit formal for Maui, but there's no disputing the level of comfort, with three swimming pools, a nine-hole putting green to complement the three nearby golf courses, ten tennis courts, spa, and croquet lawn. Prices start at $385.

Kahului

See the map on p.72 for locations of these listings.

Maui Beach Hotel 170 W Ka'ahumanu Ave ☎808/877-0051 or 1-888/649-3222, ⓦwww.elleairmaui.com. Although it's right on the oceanfront, this veteran hotel is also in the middle of Kahului's downtown business district, and following a long-overdue renovation has wisely decided to pitch itself at bargain-hunting business travelers rather than tourists. Its 150 small, simple but adequate rooms start as low as $115.

Maui Seaside Hotel 100 W Ka'ahumanu Ave ☎808/877-3311 or 1-800/560-5552, ⓦwww.mauiseasidehotel.com. Bland but reasonably well-kept waterfront hotel, with a swimming pool and its own artificial beach. The location, across from the shopping malls, is hardly romantic, but at least it is by the sea, and the *Seaside* makes a convenient and relatively inexpensive base.

Rooms that face inland start at $98, ocean-view ones at $138; for the best rates, book online.

Wailuku

See the map on p.77 for locations of these listings.

Banana Bungalow 310 N Market St ☎808/244-5090 or 1-800/846-7835, ⓦwww.mauihostel.com. Friendly independent hostel, open to non-Hawaiian residents only, located in a rundown light industrial area not far from central Wailuku. Beds in two- and three-bed dorms are $26.50, while basic private rooms, without en-suite facilities, cost from $54 single, $65 double. Guests can hang out in the gardens and living rooms. There's one free shuttle daily to the airport and to Kanahā beach, plus a changing rotation of free excursions to all parts of the island. The hostel also offers free Internet access and use of a Jacuzzi.

Northshore Hostel 2080 Vineyard St ☎808/986-8095 or 1-866/946-7835, ⓦwww.northshorehostel.com. Refurbished budget accommodation in downtown Wailuku, with communal kitchen facilities. Beds are in plain, four- and six-bed dorms and cost $25, or $20 with leaflets available at the airport, while equally plain private rooms – each with just a bed or two beds, and a closet – go for $50 single, $65 double. Popular with European travelers, who leave their surf-boards propped against the giant banyan in the courtyard.

Old Wailuku Inn at Ulupono 2199 Kaho'okele St ☎808/244-5897 or 1-800/305-4899, ⓦwww.mauiinn.com. A spacious plantation-style home, set in landscaped gardens a short walk south of central Wailuku, that's been converted into a luxurious ten-room B&B. All rooms have tasteful 1930s-era furnishings, attractive Hawaiian quilts, private *lānais*, and baths, and are equipped with DVDs; some also have whirlpool spas. The upstairs rooms enjoy good views. Guests share use of a living room and verandah, and eat a generous breakfast communally. Prices range $150–190; two-night minimum stay.

Central Maui

See the map on p.84 for the location of this listing.

The Inn at Mama's Fish House 799 Poho Place, Pā'ia ☎808/579-9764 or 1-800/860-4852, ⊛www.mamasfish house.com. Six fully equipped, tropically styled rental apartments right beside Kuau Beach, and alongside a popular restaurant. Three have two bedrooms and look out over the ocean, and cost $475; the others have one, but can still hold four guests. They're set slightly back in lush gardens, and cost $225.

Kīhei

See the map on p.92 for locations of these listings.

Aloha Pualani Hotel Boutique 15 Wailana Place ☎808/875-6990 or 1-866/870-6990, ⊛www.alohapualani .com. Five two-story suites across from Mā'alaea Bay at the north end of Kīhei, recently overhauled to more luxurious standards that start at $265. Each unit has a living room, kitchen, bedroom, and *lānai*, and they're clustered around a central pool and bar. On-site owners provide breakfast and advice. Two-night minimum stay.

Hale Kai O'Kīhei 1310 Uluniu Rd ☎808/879-7288 or 1-800/457-7014, ⊛www.hkokmaui.com; also available through Condominium Rentals Hawaii (see box, p.158). Three stories of straightforward one- and two-bedroom condos, costing from $130, in an absolutely stunning and very quiet beachfront location, near Kīhei's best malls and restaurants. There's also a private coconut grove, spacious *lānais*, and discounted car rental.

Kama'ole Nalu Resort 2450 S Kīhei Rd ☎808/879-1006 or 1-800/767-1497, ⊛www.kamaolenalu.com. Large beachfront complex set on neat lawns at the south end of Kama'ole Park 2. Two-bedroom, two-bath condos, all with kitchen and laundry facilities; the long, private *lānais* provide spectacular sunset views. Garden-view rooms start at $150, ocean views at $175. Five-night minimum stay, and discounts on car rental.

Kīhei Akahi 2531 S Kīhei Rd; available through Condominium Rentals Hawaii ☎808/879-2778 or 1-800/367-5242, ⊛www.crhmaui.com. The ascending rows of unexciting but low-priced and reasonably well-furnished condos (all capable of sleeping four) in this garden property across from Kama'ole Park 2 have use of two swimming pools and a tennis court, but no views to speak of. Rates start at $122; four-night minimum stay.

Mana Kai Maui 2960 S Kīhei Rd; available through Condominium Rentals Hawaii ☎808/879-2778 or 1-800/367-5242, ⊛www.crhmaui.com. Large building beside lovely Keawakapu Beach at the grander south end of Kīhei, with small hotel rooms starting at $175 in high season, and full-blown condo apartments from $260, plus a pool and the excellent *Five Palms Beach Grill* restaurant (see p.95).

Maui Coast Hotel 2259 S Kīhei Rd ☎808/874-6284 or 1-800/895-6284, ⊛www.mauicoasthotel.com. Tasteful, upscale, and reasonable-value modern hotel, set slightly back from the highway opposite Kama'ole Park 1. Standard hotel rooms from around $185, as well as pricier one- and two-bedroom suites, with good deals on car rental, plus an attractive pool with poolside bar, and an above-average restaurant, *Spices*.

Maui Vista 2191 S Kīhei Rd ☎808/879-7966; reserve through Marc Resorts, ☎808/922-9700 or 1-800/535-0085, ⊛www.marcresorts.com; or through Kīhei agencies listed on p.158. Comfortable, well-equipped condos of all sizes, from $132 per night, on the hillside across from Kama'ole Park 1. Not the best views, but amenities include three pools and six tennis courts.

Royal Mauian Resort 2430 S Kīhei Rd ☎808/879-1263 or 1-800/367-8009, ⊛www.royalmauianresort.com. Huge, luxurious, oceanfront condo complex, though lacking a/c, beyond the south end of Kama'ole Park 1. Highlights include the lovely views, especially from the roof terrace, and a nice pool. Rates start at $195; five-night minimum stay, and discounts on car rental.

Sunseeker Resort 551 S Kīhei Rd ☎808/879-1261 or 1-800/532-6284, ⊛www.mauisunseeker.com. This small hotel-cum-condo building, which caters to a predominantly gay clientele and offers a hair salon and massage, stands very close to Māʻalaea Bay beach (and, unfortunately, also the main road) at the north end of Kīhei. As renovated by its enthusiastic owners, it offers great-value rooms and suites from $145, all with kitchen facilities and ocean views. The cheapest rooms are in what was formerly the separate *Wailana Inn*, immediately behind; all guests can use the hot tub and deck on that building's roof. Three-night minimum stay.

Wailea and Mākena

See the map on p.99 for locations of these listings.

Fairmont Kea Lani Maui **4100 Wailea Alanui Drive** ☎808/875-4100 or 1-800/257-7544, ⓦ www.kealani.com. Locals call it the Taj Mahal, but this dazzling white resort is more like something from the Arabian Nights. Despite its flamboyant domed silhouette, the interior is characterized by smooth unadorned curves, and you can see through the lobby to lily ponds and the lagoon-cum-pool, crossed by little footbridges. Two huge wings of plush rooms (all equipped with TVs and DVD players), 37 garden villas, and some excellent restaurants are all focused on lovely Polo Beach (see p.100); there's also a great Italian deli. Rates start at $395 for a garden view, $495 for an ocean view.

Four Seasons Resort Maui at Wailea **3900 Wailea Alanui Drive** ☎808/874-8000 or 1-800/334-6284, ⓦ www.fourseasons .com/maui. Lavish resort property at the south end of Wailea, with a large, beautiful, white-sand beach on view beyond the open lobby, and a gorgeous, palm-ringed pool. Rooms have private *lānais*, bamboo furnishings, and 24-hour room service, and you can choose from several restaurants, including *Spago* (see p.106). Mountain-view rooms cost from $440, garden-view or ocean-view rooms or suites from $570.

Grand Wailea Resort **3850 Wailea Alanui Drive** ☎808/875-1234 or 1-800/888-6100, ⓦ www.grandwailea .com. Large and very ostentatious resort hotel, with a five-level swimming pool ("Wailea Canyon") that's linked by waterslides and features a swim-up bar, hot-tub grottoes, and even a water elevator back to the top. There's also a luxurious spa, half a dozen restaurants, a nightclub, and tropical flowers everywhere. The published rack rates start at $575 for a terrace view, $825 for an ocean view, but you can normally find discounts of around thirty percent online.

Maui Prince **5400 Mākena Alanui Drive** ☎808/874-1111 or 1-888/977-4623, ⓦ www.mauiprince.com. South Maui's southernmost resort is a secluded and stylish low-rise facing gorgeous, sandy Maluaka Beach, and just about within walking distance of the even more wonderful Big Beach (see p.101). The main hotel block focuses inwards around a central courtyard; the rooms are spacious, pared-down, and elegant, with prices usually available from around $250; and there are trickling ponds filled with *koi* carp everywhere you look. Top-quality Japanese and Pacific Rim restaurants, golf packages, pilates, and yoga on the beach, and early-morning snorkel cruises to nearby Molokini. Look for great room-and-car deals online.

Outrigger Palms at Wailea **3700 Wailea Alanui Drive** ☎808/879-5800 or 1-888/294-7731, ⓦ www.outrigger .com. Though Wailea's first resort hotel has been thoroughly upgraded to match its neighbors, it retains its original open-air appeal. Comprising several small buildings in landscaped gardens and a larger central tower, all with spacious, comfortable rooms, the hotel offers three pools, two restaurants, plus Hawaiiana lectures and four weekly *lūʻaus* (see p.173). The nearest beach, however, is ten minutes' walk away. Garden-view rooms officially start at $269, ocean-view ones at $295, but you can often find rates below $200.

Pineapple Inn Maui **3170 Akala Drive** ☎808/298-4403 or 1-877/212-6284, ⓦ www.pineappleinnmaui.com. Small, very comfortable purpose-built inn, high on the Wailea hillside, that makes a wonderfully affordable alternative to the giants down below. The pastel-yellow main building holds four guest rooms with private baths and ocean-view *lānais* from $119, and there's a separate two-bedroom cottage at $195.

Renaissance Wailea Beach Resort 3550 Wailea Alanui Drive ☎808/879-4900 or 1-800/992-4532, ⓦwww .renaissancehotels.com. A highly luxurious resort, stacked in seven tiers above twin crescent beaches and boasting swimming pools set amid lush gardens. Almost 350 sumptuous rooms come with DVDs and *lānais* angled towards the ocean. Those closest to the sea start at $429, while mountain views cost from $329.

Upcountry Maui

See the map on p.108 for locations of these listings.

Hale Ho'okipa 32 Pakani Place, Makawao ☎808/572-6698 ⓦwww .maui-bed-and-breakfast.com. Tucked away on a quiet residential street, this lovely timber-built plantation-style home abounds in tasteful architectural detail. Its three well furnished en-suite B&B rooms share a common living room and cost $115–160. Good breakfasts are served in a friendly atmosphere.

Kili's Cottage Kula; reserve through Hawaii's Best B&B ☎808/263-3100 or 1-800/262-9912, ⓦwww.bestbnb .com. A real bargain: a comfortable three-bedroom, two-bathroom house, set in beautiful upland gardens below Pūlehu, equipped with TV, VCR, and full kitchen, and rented for $115, less than the price of most Maui hotel rooms. Three-night minimum stay.

Kula Lodge RR1 ☎808/878-1535 or 1-800/233-1535, ⓦwww.kulalodge .com. Upmarket board and lodging in a Hawaiian approximation of an Alpine inn, *makai* of Haleakalā Highway, just before the Haleakalā Crater Road turnoff. Accommodation is in five chalets, four of which can sleep family parties: all are comfortably furnished, though they don't have phones or TV, and cost $125–185.

Malu Manu 446 Cooke Rd ☎808/878-6111 or 1-888/878-6161, ⓦwww .maui.net/~alive/. Two short-term rentals in seven acres of gardens, enjoying magnificent views, 4000 feet up the flanks of Haleakalā. Besides a fully furnished two-bedroom house costing $185, there's a smaller "writer's retreat" cabin for $150; both are furnished with antiques and share use of an outdoor hot tub. Three-night minimum stay.

Pilialoha 2512 Kaupakalua Rd, Ha'ikū ☎808/572-1440, ⓦwww.pilialoha .com. Small cottage in the gardens of a private home above Ha'ikū, with kitchen, bathroom, and space enough to sleep four comfortably. $130 per night, three-night minimum stay.

Star Lookout 622 Thompson Rd, Kula ☎808/878-6730, reservations on ☎907/346-8028, ⓦwww.starlookout .com. Gorgeous rental cottage perched high on the green Upcountry slopes just above Kula, offering comfortable accommodation for four for $200 per night. There's a full kitchen, and a long *lānai*, with stupendous views. Two-night minimum stay.

The road to Hāna

See the map on p.127 for locations of these listings.

Aloha Maui Cottages PO Box 790210, Pā'ia ☎808/572-0298, ⓦwww .alohamauicottages.com. Very rural B&B, not far off Hwy-360 thirteen miles east of Pā'ia, consisting of four simple but attractive and comfortable cabins that cost $70–135. The cheapest, which share a bathroom, are a bargain for budget travelers. The helpful owner can lend you a bike, but you'll need a car to get here. Three-night minimum.

Huelo Point Flower Farm PO Box 791808, Pā'ia ☎808/572-1850, ⓦwww .mauiflowerfarm.com. Luxury clifftop accommodation thirteen miles east of Pā'ia, with spectacular views over Waipi'o Bay, plus an on-site waterfall and open-air waterfront Jacuzzi. Two separate cottages at $300 – either of which would make a lavish, private honeymoon retreat – plus larger houses appropriate for four or six guests, costing $600.

Hāna Vacation Rentals

Hāna Ali'i Holidays (☎808/248-7742 or 1-800/548-0478, ⊛www.hanamauitravel.com) offers the choice from some twenty apartments and cottages in and around Hāna, many by the ocean, and some absolutely gorgeous. Rates range from $90 to $450 a night, but $125–150 should get you a spacious and attractive cottage.

Hāna

See the map on p.135 for locations of these listings.

Hāmoa Bay House and Bungalow PO Box 773, Hāna HI 96713 ☎808/248-7884, ⊛www.hamoabay.com. Two fabulous rental properties, splendidly isolated – even from each other – two miles south of Hāna. The bungalow rents for $225; perched on stilts in a jungle-like setting, and with an open-air Jacuzzi on its wooden *lānai*, it makes an idyllic honeymoon hideaway. The house is large enough for two couples, and costs $285. Both have Balinese bamboo furnishings, and require a three-night minimum stay.

Hāna Hale Inn 4829 Ua'kea Rd ☎808/248-7641, ⊛www.hanahaleinn.com. A cluster of distinctive rainforest-style wooden buildings, not far up from the ocean and overlooking an attractive fishpond that actually belongs to the neighbors. All are very luxurious, with hot tubs and bamboo furnishings; prices range from $145 for the Garden Suite, up to $260 for the Royal Suite, which can comfortably sleep four.

Hana Kai-Maui Resort 1533 Ua'kea Rd ☎808/248-8426 or 1-800/346-2772 (US), ⊛www.hanakaimaui.com. Small, eighteen-unit condo set in lovely multi-level gardens overlooking Hāna Bay, a short way north of Hāna Beach County Park. Each well-equipped studio and one-bedroom unit has a kitchen and private *lānai*; the larger ones sleep four. Studios for $145–196 with apartments costing between $165 and $294.

Hotel Hāna-Maui 5031 Hāna Hwy ☎808/248-8211 or 1-800/321-4262, ⊛www.hotelhanamaui.com. Secluded luxury hotel, built in the 1940s as Hawaii's first self-contained resort and integrated into the community to create a unique atmosphere. In addition to the older rooms in the Bay Cottages near the lobby, which start at $475, rows of plantation-style Sea Ranch cottages are arranged across the lawns that drop down to the ocean. They have no TVs, but boast every other creature comfort, with kitchenettes and private *lānais* that have individual hot tubs and enjoy great views; prices range up to $1075, the closer you get to the sea. As well as regular shuttles to Hāmoa Beach for activities, hotel guests have use of tennis courts and a pitch-and-putt golf course, and there's regular live music in the lounge.

Joe's Place PO Box 746, 4870 Ua'kea Rd ☎808/248-7033, ⊛www.joesrentals.com. Joe himself passed away some years ago, but his ordinary Hāna home, opposite the *Hāna Kai-Maui Resort*, still offers eight simple rooms, sharing a kitchen and communal lounge. All cost $45 except the one that has its own en-suite bath, priced at $55; there are no sea views, but this is Hāna's best option for budget travelers.

Lanai

See the map on p.148 for locations of these listings.

Four Seasons Resort Lanai, The Lodge at Kō'ele 1 Keōmoku Hwy, Lanai City HI 96763 ☎808/565-4000 or 1-800/919-5053, ⊛www.fourseasons.com/koele. Quite why *The Lodge* should win the *Condé Nast Traveler* readers' poll as the world's best tropical resort is anyone's guess, since the gorgeous, immensely luxurious hotel is several miles from the ocean, 1600ft up in a pine forest reminiscent of the Scottish Highlands. The ambience is pure country-house, and most of the one hundred rooms – tucked away in the low bungalows around the "executive putting course" and croquet lawns – are comfortably furnished rather than opulent. Guests have full privileges and

Camping

Opportunities to camp on Maui are very limited, with the best sites being in Haleakalā National Park, in and near the crater, as detailed on p.119, and also at Kīpahulu on the southeast shore, where there's a free and extremely rudimentary first-come, first-served oceanfront campground at 'Ohe'o Gulch.

There's also great oceanfront camping at Wai'ānapanapa State Park, where tent camping costs $5 per person, while basic cabins, each holding up to four people, cost $45 per cabin. Permits are available from the Department of Land and Natural Resources, 54 S High St, Wailuku, HI 96793 (Mon–Fri 8am–3.30pm; ☎808/984-8109, ⓦwww.state.hi.us/dlnr), but the cabins are usually reserved far in advance.

On Lanai, you can camp for up to a week at Hulopo'e Beach's tiny, peaceful six-pitch campground (☎808/565-3982). There's a charge of $5 per person per night, plus a one-time $5 registration fee.

beach access at the *Mānele Bay*. Rooms start at $295, which with a fourth night free is surprisingly reasonable, and range up to well over $2000.

Four Seasons Resort Lanai at Mānele Bay 1 Mānele Bay Rd, Lanai 96763; ☎808/565-2000 or 1-800/919-5053, ⓦwww.fourseasons.com/manelebay. Despite its name, the *Mānele Bay* is not actually at Mānele Bay, although its jade-tiled roof is visible from the harbor. It spreads itself instead across the hillside above the much nicer Hulopo'e Beach, a few hundred yards west. Although *The Lodge at Kō'ele* is regarded as the island's flagship hotel, the *Mānele Bay* conforms far more closely to what most visitors want from Hawaii: a lovely beach, ocean views, marble terraces, cocktails by the pool, and plenty of sun. Its 250 lavishly appointed rooms (some of which come with their own private butler) are arranged in two-story terraced buildings, engulfed by colorful gardens, with a golf course alongside. The whole property is themed towards Hawaiian and Pacific history, and centers on a wonderful pool. There's also a luxury spa, boasting Hawaiian treatments such as *lomi lomi* massage or *ti*-leaf wraps ($100 and up for 45min). Terrace-view rooms cost $400, garden- or ocean-view room $575–6500, with a fourth night free.

Hotel Lanai 828 Lānai Ave ☎808/565-7211 or 1-877/665-2624, ⓦwww.hotellanai.com. Appealing wooden bungalow hotel, perched at the edge of the woods above Dole Park. Built for Jim Dole in the 1920s, it's now run as an inexpensive, low-key alternative to the resorts, and consists of a long central verandah flanked by two wings of tasteful, comfortable but simple en-suite rooms priced at $125–145, plus a self-contained cottage costing $175. Rates include a self-service continental breakfast abounding in pineapple. There's also a good restaurant, while guests have free access to the facilities at the two resort hotels (except the pool at the *Mānele Bay Hotel*) and can make use of the same free bus services. At the time this book went to press, *Hotel Lanai* was about to change hands, however, so changes may be imminent.

Lanai Plantation Home 547 Twelfth St ☎808/565-6961 or 1-800/566-6961, ⓦwww.dreamscometruelanai.com. This restored plantation home, set in nice gardens a short walk southeast of Dole Park, has four very comfortable guest rooms, each with a luxurious en-suite bathroom, that can be rented out individually at $112, or you can also rent the entire house, costing $450.

Essentials

Arrival

All flights to **Maui** from beyond Hawaii, and the vast majority of flights from the other Hawaiian islands, land at **Kahului Airport**, a couple of miles east of Kahului on the central isthmus. All the national rental car chains are represented at the airport, and while there are no scheduled bus services, it is possible to catch a shuttle bus to wherever you're staying, with either Aloha Tours (☎808/879-2828 or 1-800/977-2605, ⓦwww.akinatours.com) or Speedishuttle (☎808/661-6667 or 1-877/242-5777, ⓦwww.speedishuttle.com). Typical rates start at around $15 to Kīhei, $28 to Lahaina, and $36 to Nāpili. Taxis are also available.

In addition, **Kapalua** in West Maui, which is much closer to the resorts of Kā'anapali and Lahaina, receives around six daily flights from Honolulu, while local commuter services also land at tiny Hāna airport in East Maui.

Hawaii's long-awaited **Super Ferry** system (☎1-877/443-3779, ⓦwww.hawaiisuperferry.com), connecting Honolulu, on the island of Oahu, with Kahului Harbor on Maui, started operations in the fall of 2007. However, services during the opening months were repeatedly suspended, due both to legal challenges from environmentalists, and to problems with the boat itself. Assuming that the political battles are over, and the ferry proves economically viable, a huge catamaran, capable of carrying cars and trucks, leaves Honolulu at 6.30am daily, arrives at Kahului at 10.15am, and then sails back from Kahului to Oahu at 11.15am. One-way fares start at $39 per passenger, plus $55 per vehicle, though fuel surcharges mean that the trip for a car with two adults typically costs almost $300. In addition, separate ferries connect Lahaina with Lanai and Molokai; see p.170.

Information

The best source of visitor information on Maui is the local "chapter", as it's called, of the **Hawaii Visitors Bureau** (☎808/244-3530 or 1-800/525-MAUI, ⓦwww.visitmaui.com). Their website holds links to all sorts of island operators and agencies, and you can also use it to order a copy of their glossy guide-cum-directory to the island, though in truth it consists largely of advertisements. Their main office on the island itself, tucked away half a mile northeast of central Wailuku at 1727 Wili Pa Loop (Mon–Fri 8am–4.30pm), stocks plenty more printed material.

In West Maui, the Lahaina Visitor Center, inside the Old Lahaina Court House on Banyan Tree Square (daily 9am–5pm; ☎808/667-9193 or 1-888/310-1117, ⓦwww.visitlahaina.com), stocks a small array of brochures and leaflets, though it's more of an official souvenir store than a useful resource.

You'll find **websites** for accommodation, activities and all kinds of other things listed throughout this book. Otherwise, the most useful site for Maui as a whole is ⓦwww.maui.net, an all-purpose Maui portal featuring links to accommodation agencies, individual properties, activities, and local newspapers like the *Maui News* (ⓦwww.mauinews.com) and *Haleakalā Times* (ⓦwww.haleakalatimes.com).

Getting Around

It's virtually impossible to make the most of a Maui vacation without renting your own vehicle, but the island does offer a rudimentary public transport network.

Driving on Maui

In the absence of adequate roads to cope with its volume of tourists, the **traffic** on Maui is consistently bad. The worst areas are the woefully inadequate Mokulele Highway between Kīhei and Kahului, and the narrow Honoapiʻilani Highway around West Maui, where drivers habitually make sudden stops in winter to whale watch. At least the snail's pace along the Haleakalā and Hāna highways is due to the natural obstacles en route, and gives you a chance to appreciate the scenery. Rental companies forbid their clients to drive off-road, which can lead to trouble if you're heading for obscure beaches or surf sites. In the past, those strictures have applied to both the Kahekili Highway in West Maui, and the remote Piʻilani Highway along the southern coast of East Maui (closed when this book went to press; see p.145), but they seldom do so any longer.

All the national **rental car chains** are represented at Kahului Airport and at or near Kapalua Airport; in addition, Avis has branches in Kīhei, Wailea, and Kapalua; Budget has an office in Wailea; and Dollar is in Hāna.

Buses

Maui Bus (☎ 808/871-4838, ⓦ www .mauicounty.gov/bus) operates sched-uled **bus** services from the Queen Kaʻahumanu Center in Kahului to Lahaina ($1; departs Kahului daily 5.30am–7.30pm, Wharf Cinema Center in Lahaina daily 6.30am–8.30pm), and also to both **Kīhei** and **Wailea** ($1; departs Kahului daily 5.30am–7.30pm, the Shops At Wailea daily 6.30am–8.30pm). Both routes run via the Maui Ocean Center at Māʻalaea, meaning that with one change of bus you can get from Lahaina to Wailea.

More local routes also connect **Kahului airport** with downtown Kahului and Pāʻia and Haikū; Lahaina with Kāʻanapali (departs Lahaina Harbor daily 6.30am–8.30pm); and Kīhei's Piʻilani Shopping Center with **Māʻalaea** ($1; departs Kīhei daily 4.53am–7.53pm).

Cycling

Among companies renting out **mountain bikes**, typically at $25–30 per day or up to $120 per week, are South Maui Bicycles, 1993 S Kīhei Rd, Kīhei (☎ 808/874-0068, ⓦ www.stirflux.com /smb); West Maui Cycles, 1087 Limahana Place, Lahaina (☎ 808/661-9005, ⓦ www.westmauicycles.com); and Island Biker, 415 Dairy Rd, Kahului (☎ 808/877-7744, ⓦ www.islandbiker.com). Chris' Bike Adventures (☎ 808/871-2453) can arrange customized bike **tours** of Maui. A full list of operators running **downhill bike rides** on Haleakalā appears on p.178.

Ferries

The Superferry services between Oahu and Maui are detailed on p.169. In addition, Lahaina Harbor is home to a couple of **inter-island ferry services**. *Expeditions* (☎ 808/661-3756 or, from outside Maui, 1-800/695-2624, ⓦ www .go-lanai.com) sails from in front of the *Pioneer Inn* to Manele Bay on **Lanai** daily at 6.45am, 9.15am, 12.45pm, 3.15pm, and 5.45pm. Departures from Lanai are at 8am, 10.30am, 2pm, 4.30pm, and 6.45pm; the adult fare is $25 each way, while under-12s go for $20. The trip takes approximately fifty minutes. It's also possible to make a 1hr 30min ferry crossing between Maui and **Molokai** on the *Molokai Princess* (adults $40 one-way, children $20; ☎ 808/662-3535 or 1-877/500-6284, ⓦ www.mauiprin-cess.com). The boat leaves Lahaina at 7.15am and 6pm daily, and returns from Kaunakakai Harbor on Molokai at 5.30am and 4pm.

Money

Although it's possible to have an inexpensive vacation on Maui, there's no getting away from the fact that prices in Hawaii are consistently higher – on the scale of around forty percent – than in the rest of the United States. Locals call it the "Paradise Tax" – the price you pay for living in paradise.

Average costs

How much you spend each day is, of course, up to you, but it's hard to get any sort of breakfast for under $8, a cheap lunch can easily come to $15, and an evening meal in a restaurant, with drinks, is likely to cost $30 or more per person, even if you're trying to economize.

As outlined in the accommodation section, Maui has a couple of hostels (in Wailuku), which charge around $25 for a dorm bed, but otherwise even the cheapest hotels and B&Bs tend to charge at least $100 a night for a double room, and a rental car with gas won't cost less than $30 a day. It's easy to spend $100 per person per day before you've done anything: pay for a snorkel cruise, let alone a helicopter ride, and you've cleared $150.

A state **sales tax** of 4.166 percent is imposed on all transactions. Hotels impose an additional 7.25 percent tax, adding a total of 11.42 percent to accommodation bills.

Money and Banks

Most visitors find that there's no reason to carry large amounts of cash or travelers' checks to Hawaii. Automatic teller machines (**ATMs**), which accept cards issued by most domestic and foreign banks, can be found almost everywhere; call your own bank if you're in any doubt. The two major **banks** are the Bank of Hawaii, which belongs to the Plus network of ATMs, and the First Hawaiian Bank, which belongs to the Plus and Cirrus networks. Even the smallest town tends to hold a branch of one or the other.

If you do want to take **traveler's checks** – which offer the great security of knowing that lost or stolen checks will be replaced – be sure to get them issued in US dollars. Foreign currency, whether cash or traveler's checks, can be hard to exchange, so foreign travelers should change some of their money into dollars at home.

For most services, it's taken for granted that you'll be paying with a **credit card**. Hotels and car rental companies routinely require an imprint of your card whether or not you intend to use it to pay.

Food and Drink

Gone are the days when the Hawaiian islands were self-sufficient Gardens of Eden; the state now produces less than twenty percent of the food it consumes, and in many ways eating in Maui can be much like eating anywhere else in the US.

However, two important factors work in favor of visitors hoping for memorable culinary experiences. First of all, there's the island's ethnic diversity. Immigrants from all over the world have brought their own national dishes and recipes to Hawaii, and those separate traditions have repeatedly mingled to create intriguing new cuisines. Second, the presence of thousands of tourists, many prepared to pay top rates for good food, means that the island holds some truly superb fine dining restaurants, run by internationally renowned chefs.

Note that all restaurants are now obliged by law to **forbid smoking**.

Local restaurants

Maui has its fair share of outlets of the national fast-food chains, but locally owned budget restaurants, diners and takeout stands serve a hybrid cuisine that draws on the traditions of Japan, China, Korea and the Philippines as well as the US mainland. The resultant mixture has a slight but definite Hawaiian twist. In fact, the term "local" food has a distinct meaning in Hawaii, and specifically applies to this multi-cultural melange.

Breakfast tends to be the standard combination of eggs, meat, pancakes, muffins or toast. At midday, the usual dish is the plate lunch, a molded tray holding meat and rice as well as potato or macaroni salad and costing from $6 to $9; *bento* is the Japanese equivalent, with mixed meats and rice, while in Filipino diners you'll be offered *adobo*, pork or chicken stewed with garlic and vinegar. Korean barbecue, *kal bi* – prepared with sesame – is especially tasty, while **saimin** (pronounced *sy-min*), a bowl of clear soup filled with noodles and other ingredients, has become something of a national dish. Finally, the carbohydrate-packed *loco moco* is a fried egg served on a hamburger with gravy and rice.

Food in general is often referred to as *kaukau*, and it's also worth knowing that *pupus* (pronounced *poo-poos*) is a general term for little snacks, the kind of finger food that is given away in early-evening happy hours.

Lū'aus

These days, there's no such thing as an authentic "Hawaiian" restaurant; the closest you can come to eating traditional foods is at a **lū'au**. Primarily tourist money-spinners, and always accompanied by pseudo-Polynesian entertainment, these offer the chance to sample such dishes as *kālua* pork, an entire pig wrapped in *ti* leaves and baked all day in an underground oven; *poke*, which is raw fish, shellfish or octopus, marinated with soy and oriental seasonings; *poi*, a purple-gray paste produced

Hawaiian fish

Although the ancient Hawaiians were expert offshore fishermen, as well as being sophisticated fish farmers, the great majority of the **fish** eaten in Hawaii nowadays is imported. Thus the salmon and crab featured on menus here come from Alaska, and the mussels from New Zealand. However, if you feel like being adventurous, you should get plenty of opportunity to try some of the Pacific species caught nearby. If the list below still leaves you in the dark, top recommendations include *opah*, which is chewy and salty like swordfish; the chunky *'ōpakapaka*, which because of its red color (associated with happiness) is often served on special occasions; the succulent white *ono* (which means "delicious" in Hawaiian); and the dark *'ahi*, the most popular choice for sashimi.

'ahi	yellow-fin tuna	*onaga*	red snapper
a'u	swordfish or marlin	*ono*	mackerel or tuna-like fish
'ehu	red snapper	*'ōpae*	shrimp
hāpu'upu'u	sea bass	*opah*	moonfish
hebi	spear fish	*ōpakapaka*	pink snapper
kalekale	pink snapper	*uhu*	parrot fish
mahimahi	dorado or dolphin fish	*'uku*	gray snapper
mano	shark	*ulua*	jack fish
moi	thread fish		

by pounding the root of the *taro* plant; and *lomi-lomi*, a dish made with raw salmon. As *lū'aus* always involve mass catering and canteen-style self-service, the food itself, with the exception of Lahaina's *Feast At Lele*, is not sufficient incentive to go.

Drums of the Pacific, *Hyatt Regency Maui*, Kā'anapali ☎808/661-1234. Daily. $89. See p.64.

The Feast at Lele, 505 Front St, Lahaina ☎808/667-5353, ⓦwww.feastatlele.com. Daily. $105. See p.58.

Maui Sunset Lū'au, *Maui Prince*, Mākena ☎808/875-5888. Tues & Thurs. $83. See p.106.

Old Lahaina Lū'au, Lahaina Cannery Mall, Lahaina ☎808/667-1998, ⓦwww .oldlahainaluau.com. Daily. $89. See p.60.

Royal Lahaina Lū'au, *Royal Lahaina Resort*, Kā'anapali ☎808/661-9119, ⓦwww.lahainaluau.com. Daily. $86.

Wailea's Finest Lū'au, *Outrigger Palms at Wailea*, Wailea ☎808/879-1922. Mon & Thurs–Sat 5pm. $85.

Fine dining

Many of Maui's **best restaurants** are in its most expensive hotels, and a meal in the showcase resorts of Kā'anapali and Wailea can cost as much as $100 per head. However, less exclusive communities such as Lahaina, Kīhei, and Pā'ia all manage to support a wide range of excellent eating options at more affordable prices. In the last few years, a distinctive Hawaiian cuisine has begun to emerge, known variously as **Pacific Rim**, **Euro-Asian**, or **Hawaii Regional**. In its ideal form it consists of combining foods and techniques from all the countries and ethnic groups that have figured in Hawaiian history, using the freshest ingredients possible. Top chefs, like Roy Yamaguchi of *Roy's*, preserve natural flavors by flash-frying meat and fish like the Chinese, baking it whole like the Hawaiians or even serving it raw like the Japanese. The effect is enhanced with Thai herbs and spices, and by the inventiveness of modern Californian cooking.

Maui also has plenty of conventional **American** shrimp and steak specialists, as well as high-class **Italian**, **Thai** and **Chinese** places. Many restaurants offer all-you-can-eat **buffets** one or more nights of the week; they all sacrifice quality to quantity, so you might as well go for the cheaper ones. Lastly, to cater for that much-prized customer, the Japanese big-spender, some large hotels have very good Japanese restaurants.

Drink

The usual range of wines (mostly Californian, though Maui does have its own Tedeschi Winery; see p.112) and beers is sold at Maui restaurants and bars. At some point, however, every visitor seems to insist on getting wiped out by a **tropical cocktail** or two. Among the most popular are the Mai Tai, which should contain at least two kinds of rum, together with orange curacao and lemon juice; the Blue Hawaii, in which vodka is colored with blue curacao; and the Planter's Punch, made with light rum, grenadine, bitters and lemon juice.

Tap water is safe to drink. If you're hiking, however, never drink untreated stream water.

Tours

Bus Tours

The most popular **bus tours** on the island run around East Maui to Hāna (typically costing $80–100 per person), and up the volcano to Haleakalā Crater (more like $70–80). Operators include Akina Aloha Tours (☎808/879-2828, ⓦwww.akinatours.com), Polynesian Adventure Tours (☎808/877-4242 or 1-800/622-3011, ⓦwww.polyad.com), and Ekahi Tours (☎ 808/877-9775 or 1-888/292-2422, ⊛ www.ekahi.com).

Flight-seeing tours

Helicopter **flight-seeing tours** are firmly established as a must-do activity for any visitor to Hawaii. A full round-island flight over Maui, which will enable you to see such wonders as Haleakalā Crater and the summit of the West Maui mountains from above, takes more than an hour and cost around $200 per person. If you'd prefer a shorter flight, try a 20- or 30-minute loop over West Maui.

Aim to pay around $75 for a 20-minute jaunt, something over $150 to fly over Haleakalā and Hāna, and more than $200 to fly over to Molokai or Lanai as well. Visibility is almost always best in the early morning. All the helicopter companies listed below run tours from Kahului Airport; none currently operates from Kapalua. Blue Hawaiian, which use the ultra-quiet ECO-Star helicopters, are particularly recommended.

It's also possible to take an airplane or "fixed-wing" tour, with Volcano Air Tours (☎ 808/877-5500, ⊛ www.volcano airtours.com), which flies across to the active volcano on the Big Island from Kapalua or Kahului for around $300.

Air Mau ☎ 808/877-7005 or 1-877/238-4942, ⊛ www.airmaui.com
Alexair Helicopters ☎ 808/871-0792 or 1-888/418-8455, ⊛ www.helitour.com
Blue Hawaiian Helicopters ☎ 808/871-8844 or 1-800/745-2583, ⊛ www.blue hawaiian.com
MauiScape ☎ 808/877-7272, ⊛ www .mauiscape.com
Sunshine Helicopters ☎ 808/871-5600 or 1-800/469-3000, ⊛ www.sunshine helicopters.com

Lahaina Kāʻanapali Railroad

Also known as the Sugar Cane Train, the **Lahaina Kāʻanapali Railroad** (adults $21 round-trip, under-13s $15; ☎ 808/667-6851 or, in the US only, 1-800/499-2307, ⊛ www.sugarcanetrain .com) is a restored locomotive (complete with "singing conductor") that runs six-mile, half-hour excursions through the cane fields along the tracks of the old Lahaina & Kāʻanapali Railroad. It travels from Lahaina to Kāʻanapali and then half a mile beyond to turn around at Puʻukoliʻi. For anyone other than a small child, it's not an exciting trip. The first departure from Lahaina is at 11.05am daily and the last at 4pm; from Kāʻanapali, the first is at 10.25am daily, the last at 3.10pm. There's also a weekly dinner train, setting off from Puʻukoliʻi at 5pm on Thursday (adults $79, under-13s $49). Free shuttle buses connect the Lahaina and Kāʻanapali stations with the Wharf Cinema Center and the Whalers Village, respectively.

Ocean Sports

With average water temperatures of between 75°F and 82°F (24–28°C), the sea in Maui is ideal for **ocean sports.** These range from snorkeling and scuba diving to fishing and whale watching, as well as Hawaii's greatest gift to the world, the art of surfing.

Surfing

Surf aficionados rate several Maui sites as equal to anything on Oahu's fabled North Shore, with Honolua Bay on the northern tip of West Maui, and Jaws off Haʻikū in the east (see p.128), as the greatest of all. You need to be a true expert to join the locals who surf there, however – beginners would do better to start out at Lahaina and Kāʻanapali beaches. The peak season is between November and March.

Companies that offer surfing lessons in the Lahaina area include the Goofy Foot Surf School (☎ 808/244-9283, ⊛ www .goofyfootsurfschool.com) and the Nancy

Beach safety

It's all too easy, however, to forget that Hawaiian **beaches** can be deadly as well as beautiful, and you need to know exactly what you're doing before you enter the water.

Unless you have local expertise, it's safest to swim at the official beach parks and most popular spots, especially those that are shielded by offshore reefs. Not all beaches have lifeguards and warning flags, and unattended beaches are not necessarily safe. Look for other bathers, but whatever your experience elsewhere, don't assume you'll be able to cope with the same conditions as the local kids. Always ask for advice and above all follow the cardinal rule – Never turn your back on the water.

The beaches that have the most accidents and drownings, such as Big Beach south of Mākena, tend to be those where waves of four feet or more break directly onto the shore. This varies according to the season, so beaches that are idyllic in summer can be storm-tossed death traps between October and April. If you get caught in a rip current or undertow and find yourself being dragged out to sea, stay calm and remember that the vast majority of such currents disappear within a hundred yards of the shore. Allow yourself to be carried out until the force weakens, and then swim first to one side and then back to the shore.

No one owns any stretch of beach in Hawaii. Every beach in the state – defined as the area below the vegetation line – is regarded as public property. That doesn't mean that you're entitled to stroll across any intervening land between the ocean and the nearest highway; always use the clearly signposted "public right of way" footpaths. Whatever impression the large oceanfront hotels may attempt to convey, they can't stop you from using the beaches out front; they can only restrict, but not refuse to supply, parking places for non-guests.

ESSENTIALS Ocean Sports

Emerson School of Surfing (☎808/244-7873, ⓦ www.mauisurfclinics.com). South Maui instructors include Hawaiian Style Surf School (☎808/874-0110), while Maui Waveriders (☎808/875-4761, ⓦ www.mauiwaveriders.com) operate in both locations.

Windsurfing

Maui is renowned as the world's most sublime **windsurfing** destination. Legendary Hoʻokipa Beach Park, just east of Pāʻia on the central isthmus, is a mecca for devotees and plays host to major championships throughout most of the year.

Strong winds are of greater importance to windsurfers than high surf, so summer is the peak season for the sport. Between December and February the winds tend to drop for days on end, but even then conditions are usually good enough

somewhere on the island; Māʻalaea Bay on the south shore of the isthmus is the likeliest spot.

The best place to learn to windsurf is Kanahā Beach near Kahului, a few miles west of Hoʻokipa. Expect to pay around $80 for a 2hr 30min lesson (including equipment rental) with operators such as Action Sports Maui (☎808/871-5857, ⓦ www.actionsportsmaui.com), Alan Cadiz's HST Windsurfing School (☎808/871-5423 or 1-800/968-5423, ⓦ www.hstwindsurfing.com), Hawaiian Island Surf & Sport (☎808/871-4981 or 1-800/231-6958, ⓦ www.hawaiian island.com), or Maui Ocean Activities (☎ 808/667-2001, ⓦ www .mauiwatersports.com). Maui Windsurfari specializes in putting together all-inclusive packages for windsurfers (☎808/871-7766 or 1-800/736-6284, ⓦ www.windsurfari.com).

ESSENTIALS

Ocean Sports

Discount activities

Activities operators in all the tourist areas, especially along Front Street in Lahaina, offer cut-price deals well below the advertised rates. Tom Barefoot's Cashback Tours – at 250 Alamaha St, Kahului (☎ 1-800/895-2040, ✆ www.tombarefoot.com) – is one of the few that don't also try to sell time-shares, and its website details every imaginable island activity, along with the latest prices.

Snorkeling

Maui offers some of the finest conditions for **snorkeling** in all Hawaii. Although the volcanic islet of Molokini is the most unusual and compelling destination, you can only get there if you pay for a snorkel cruise (see opposite), while plenty of great alternatives are accessible by car. When conditions are calm, the turquoise waters of magnificent Honolua Bay, at the northern tip of West Maui, are teeming with fish, while the rocky shores of La Pérouse Bay, at the southern tip of South Maui, are preserved as a marine sanctuary and offer almost infinite scope for underwater exploration. Even in the major resorts the snorkeling can be great, including the beaches at Kā'anapali and Wailea.

Diving

Maui and its immediate neighbors offer probably the best **scuba diving** in the Hawaiian islands. The most popular spots are in the vicinity of Molokini Crater, off South Maui. Learners and inexperienced divers start by exploring the sheltered, shallow "Inside Crater" area, and eventually progress to the "Back Wall," with its huge drop-offs. There's also good shore diving at Black Rock in Kā'anapali and in La Pérouse Bay, while the most spectacular dives of all lie off southern Lanai, within easy reach of a day's boat-trip from Maui.

A huge number of companies arrange diving excursions in the waters off Maui and Lanai, with the largest operator being Maui Dive Shop; full listings appear below. Prices generally start at around $80 for a one-tank trip, $100 for two tanks, with equipment rental costing an additional $25 or so. Almost all offer multi-day packages for beginners, leading to PADI certification; a typical price would be $220–250 for three days, and $300 for four. Bear in mind that many of the Molokini snorkel cruises listed opposite offer diving as well as snorkeling.

Be sure not to dive within 24 hours of flying or ascending to any significant altitude. The summit of Haleakalā is certainly out of bounds, while you should ask your dive operator for advice before even driving into the Upcountry.

Dive operators

Ed Robinson's Diving Adventures Kīhe ☎ 808/879-3584, ✆ www.mauiscuba.com
Extended Horizons Lahaina ☎ 1-888/348-3628, ✆ www.scubadivemaui.com
Maui Dive Shop Island-wide ☎ 808/879-1775, ✆ www.mauidiveshop.com
Maui Dreams Kīhei ☎ 808/874-5332, ✆ www.mauidreamdiveco.com
Mike Severn's Kīhei ☎ 808/879-6596, ✆ www.mikeseversdiving.com
Pacific Dive Lahaina ☎ 808/667-5331, ✆ www.pacificdive.com
Prodiver Kīhei ☎ 808/875-4004, ✆ prodivermaui.com
Trilogy Lahaina ☎ 1-888/225-6284, ✆ www.sailtrilogy.com

Parasailing

Parasailing, which is a bit like water-skiing, except you suddenly find yourself several hundred feet up in the air, has become very popular in the waters just off Kā'anapali and Lahaina in West Maui. To avoid disturbing humpback whales, however, it's only permitted between mid-May and mid-December. Expect to pay $45–55 for a fifteen-minute flight with operators such as Parasail Kā'anapali (☎ 808/669-6555), UFO Parasail (☎ 808/661-7836 or 1-800/359-4836, ✆ www.ufoparasailing.com), and Lahaina West Maui Parasail (☎ 808/661-4060).

Boat tours

Atlantis Submarines ☎808/667-2224 or 1-800/548-6262, ⓦwww.atlantis adventures.com. One-hour underwater excursions off Lahaina ($80; look for discounts online).

Maui Princess ☎808/661-8397 or 1-877/500-6284, ⓦwww.mauiprincess. com. Dinner ($84) and whale-watching ($27 and $34) cruises from Lahaina, plus one-day excursions to Molokai (from $80).

Pacific Whale Foundation ☎808/249-8811 or 1-800/942-5311, ⓦwww .pacificwhale.org. This nonprofit organization offers 2–3hr whale-watching cruises from Lahaina or Māʻalaea (Nov–April; $20 and $32), plus snorkeling and dolphin-watching tours to Molokini ($55–80) or Lanai ($80).

Reefdancer ☎808/667-2133. Sixty- or ninety-minute cruises ($33/$45) in a semi-submersible from Lahaina; passengers view the reef from an underwater cabin.

Trilogy Ocean Sports ☎808/661-4743 or 1-888/225-6284, ⓦwww.sailtrilogy .com. Day-long sailing trips from Lahaina to Lanai, including snorkeling, beach barbecue, and Lanai van tour ($179). They also offer diving and snorkeling at Molokini and off Lanai.

Kayak tours

Kelii's Kayak Tours ☎1-888/874-7652, ⓦwww.keliiskayak.com. Two-hour kayak tours ($54) from Lahaina, plus several more options in West, North and South Maui.

South Pacific Kayaks Rainbow Mall, 2439 S Kīhei Rd ☎808/875-4848 or 1-800/776-2326, ⓦwww.southpacific kayaks.com. An extensive range of kayaking tours, from 2hr 15min whale-watching trips ($65; in season only) via 3hr guided excursions at Mākena or Lahaina, up to extended tours in South or West Maui for up to $99.

Molokini snorkel cruises

Maui's best-known snorkeling and diving spot is the tiny crescent of **Molokini**, three miles off Mākena. Created by a volcanic eruption 230,000 years ago, it consists of half of a once-circular crater wall, poking 162ft above the waves. There's no beach or landfall of any kind, but it's a real thrill to enter the water, and see the steep crater wall dropping far into the abyss beneath you, and you're certain to see a staggering array of multi-colored fish, including deep-water species.

Countless cruises leave early each morning from Māʻalaea Harbor. It's also possible to take a significantly longer and more expensive cruise from Lahaina, while the very shortest crossing departs from Mākena's *Maui Prince* hotel (see p.163).

All the companies listed below operate out of Māʻalaea. Snorkelers can pay anything from $50 to $110 for a five- to six-hour morning trip, depending on the size and comfort of the boat and the refreshments offered, and from $35 for a shorter afternoon jaunt; scuba divers pay around $40 extra. Between November and April, many companies stop running Molokini trips and concentrate on lucrative whale-watching cruises instead.

Boat	Phone	ⓦwww.	Passengers
Four Winds II	☎808/879-8188	mauicharters.com	130
Frogman II	☎808/661-3333	bossfrog.com	52
Hokua	☎808/249-2583	alohabluecharters.com	20
Lahaina Princess	☎877/500-6284	mauiprincess.com	100
Lani Kai	☎808/244-1979	mauisnorkeling.com	70
Ocean Odyssey	☎808/249-8811	pacificwhale.org	149
Ocean Spirit	☎808/249-8811	pacificwhale.org	142
Paragon II	☎808/244-2087	sailmaui.com	35
Pride of Maui	☎808/242-0955	prideofmaui.com	140
Prince Kuhio	☎808/242-8777	mvprince.com	149
Quicksilver	☎808/661-3333	bossfrog.com	142

Equipment rental

Auntie Snorkel 2439 S Kīhei Rd, Kīhei ☎808/879-6263 or 1-877/256-4248, ⊛www.auntiesnorkel.com. Choose from snorkels and kayaks.

Boss Frog's Dive Shop 1215 S Kīhei Rd, Kīhei (☎808/891-0077); 2395 S Kīhei Rd, Kīhei (☎808/875-4477); 150 Lahainaluna Rd, Lahaina (☎808/661-3333); 3636 Lower Honoapi'ilani Rd, Kā'anapali (☎808/665-1200); 4310 Lower Honoapi'ilani Rd, Kahana (☎808/669-6700); and Nāpili Plaza, Nāpili (☎808/669-4949); ⊛www.bossfrog.com. Activity center that also rents out scuba, snorkeling, and surf gear.

Maui Dive Shop. 1455 S Kīhei Rd, Kīhei (☎808/879-3388); Honokōwai Marketplace, 3350 Lower Honoapi'ilani Rd (☎808/661-6166); and five other Maui locations; ⊛www.mauidiveshop.com. Dive

specialists who rent scuba and snorkeling equipment.

Snorkel Bob's 1279 S Kīhei Rd, Kīhei (☎808/875-6188); 2411 S Kīhei Rd, Kīhei (☎808/879-7449); Dickenson Square, Dickenson St, Lahaina (☎808/662-0104); and *Nāpili Village Hotel*, 5425C Lower Honoapi'ilani Rd, Nāpili (☎808/669-9603); ⊛www.snorkelbob.com. Snorkel gear that can be returned to any outlet on this or any other Hawaiian island.

South Pacific Kayaks Rainbow Mall, 2439 S Kīhei Rd ☎808/875-4848, ⊛www.southpacifickayaks.com. Choose from kayaks, surfboards, snorkels, boogie boards, beach chairs, and the like.

West Maui Cycles 1087 Limahana Place, Lahaina ☎808/661-9005, ⊛www.westmauicycles.com. Besides mountain bikes, you'll find snorkels, boogie boards, and surfboards.

Land Activities

Downhill biking

For over twenty years, one of Maui's most unusual and popular tourist activities has been to take a minivan to the top of Haleakalā – especially at dawn – and then climb onto a **bike** and ride, or rather roll, back down the mountain. With nearly 100,000 people making the descent each year, however, safety concerns have grown. Following a spate of serious injuries when riders came off the corkscrewing highway, and three deaths due to collisions with vehicles, the National Park Service decided in late 2007 to ban commercial operators from

running cycle trips within the park. The situation is pending review, and summit tours may conceivably resume within the lifetime of this book, but at the time of publication all the downhill biking companies were obliged to start the cycling segment of their tours 3500 feet below the summit, at the park entrance. Participants are still taken to the summit by van, but they're then driven back down again, and put on bikes at the 6500-foot level. It's undeniably less of a thrill these days, but there are advantages – it's not as seriously cold there as it is at the summit, and actually for

---

Bike tour operators

Cruiser Phil's ☎808/893-2332 or 1-877/764-2453, ⊛www.cruiserphil.com.
Maui Downhill ☎808/871-2155 or 1-800/535-2453, ⊛www.mauidownhill.com.
Maui Mountain Cruisers ☎808/871-6014 or 1-800/232-6284, ⊛www.mauimountaincruisers.com.
Mountain Riders Bike Tours ☎808/242-9739 or 1-800/706-7700, ⊛www.mountainriders.com.
Aloha Bike Tours ☎808/249-0911 or 1-800/749-1564, ⊛www.mauibike.com.
Haleakalā Bike Co ☎808/575-9575 or 1-888/922-2453, ⊛www.bikemaui.com.

most people riding twenty miles down to Makawao, or the full 28 miles all the way to the ocean on a bike. Bear in mind that taking a sunrise tour necessitates a very early start. Hotel pick-ups can be as early as 2am – hardly conducive to a happy family atmosphere.

If you're a keen cyclist back home, you may find it oddly unsatisfying that you almost never have to pedal, while the usual requirement for groups to ride together, at the pace of the slowest member, can be frustrating. If so, you might prefer to take your trip with the *Haleakalā Bike* Co (see below), based in Ha'ikū which allows cyclists to ride independently on whatever roads they choose.

The usual activities desks, such as Tom Barefoot's (see p.176) offer discount rates on biking trips: typical rates range from around $85 for a daytime ride up to $130 to go at sunrise. Unguided trips, or shorter routes, cost about $20 less. All riders must have at least some biking experience, and be aged 12 or over; all the companies supply protective gear.

Horse riding

Ironwood Ranch ☎808/669-4991, ⓦwww.ironwoodranch.com. Riding excursions up to the forest above Kapalua, at $60 for 1hr (available seasonally), $90 for 1hr 30min, $120 for 2hr, or $300 for the advanced "Ironwood Odyssey".

Mākena Stables ☎808/879-0244, ⓦwww.makenastables.com. Two- to three-hour morning or evening rides along the coastline from 'Āhihi Bay, south of Big Beach, to La Pérouse; $145–170. No credit cards. Mon–Sat.

Maui Horseback Tours ☎808/248-7799, ⓦwww.mauistables.com. Three-hour riding tours with an emphasis on Hawaiian history and spirituality, in the remote but beautiful Kīpahulu district, west of 'Ohe'o Gulch in East Maui. Departs 9.30am and 1pm daily, $150.

Mendes Ranch ☎808/871-5222, ⓦwww.mendesranch.com. Half-day tours of this cattle ranch in East Maui's Waihe'e Valley, with barbecue lunch; $130 per person or $280 with a 30min helicopter flight. Mon–Sat.

Lahaina Stables ☎808/667-2222, ⓦwww.mauihorse.com. Horseback adventures on the slopes of the West Maui mountains above Lahaina; two-hour morning rides for $110 or sunset rides for $120, 3hr 30min morning rides for $135.

Pony Express Tours ☎808/667-2200, ⓦwww.ponyexpresstours.com. 1hr 30min ($90) or 2hr ($105) tours of Haleakalā Ranch, Maui's largest cattle ranch (Mon–Fri), or 5hr 30min descent to Ka Moa O Pele junction in Haleakalā Crater ($175), with picnic lunch (Mon–Sat).

Hang-gliding

Hang Gliding Maui is a one-man operation that provides powered **hang-gliding** lessons from Hāna airport in East Maui, at $130 for 30min, $220 for 1hr (☎808/572-6557, ⓦwww.hangglidingmaui.com). The most popular spot for experienced practitioners to do some traditional hang-gliding is Polipoli State Park in the Upcountry (see p.109).

Skyline

One of Maui's most enjoyable outdoor attractions is based in the Upcountry, 2.5 miles up Haleakalā Crater Road from the point where it leaves Hwy-377. With Skyline Eco Adventures, you hike into the woodlands of Haleakalā Ranch, where you're harnessed up to ride a succession of lengthy "ziplines" across remote gullies. It's a truly breathtaking experience, though you'll have to have a head for heights to be prepared to take the initial death-defying leap ($79; ☎808/878-8400, ⓦwww.skylinehawaii.com).

ATV tours

From the same base as Skyline Eco Adventures, Haleakalā ATV Tours (☎808/661-0288, ⓦwww.atvmaui.com) offers **off-road tours** of Haleakalā Ranch in all-terrain vehicles. Three-hour tours (daily 8.30am & 12.30pm) include a brief rainforest hike and cost $129, while two-hour tours (daily 9am & 1pm) cost $95. For a slightly lower fee, you can take the same tour in the support truck rather than riding your own vehicle.

ESSENTIALS

Golf

Maui Golf courses

	Area	Holes	Kind	Fee	Phone
Dunes at Maui Lani	Kahului	18	Public	$110	☎808/873-0422
Elleair Golf Course	Kīhei	18	Public	$120	☎808/874-0777
Kāʻanapali Golf Course					
North Course	Kāʻanapali	18	Resort	$205	☎808/661-3691
South Course	Kāʻanapali	18	Resort	$170	☎808/661-3691
Kahili Golf Club	Waikapū	18	Public	$110	☎808/242-4653
Kapalua Golf Club					
Bay Course	Kapalua	18	Resort	$215	☎808/669-8044
Plantation Course	Kapalua	18	Resort	$295	☎808/669-8044
Mākena Golf Club					
North Course	Mākena	18	Resort	$190	☎808/879-3344
South Course	Mākena	18	Resort	$190	☎808/879-3344
Maui Country Club	Pāʻia	9	Private	$38	☎808/877-0616
Pukalani Country Club	Upcountry	18	Public	$68	☎808/572-1314
Waiʻehu Municipal Golf Course	Wailuku	18	Municipal	$40	☎808/243-7400
Wailea Golf Club					
Blue Course	Wailea	18	Resort	$185	☎808/875-7450
Emerald Course	Wailea	18	Resort	$200	☎808/875-7450
Gold Course	Wailea	18	Resort	$200	☎808/875-7450
Lanai					
Cavendish Municipal Golf Course	Lānaʻi City	9	Municipal	free	No phone
The Challenge at Mānele	Mānele Bay	18	Resort	$225	☎808/565-2222
The Experience at Kōʻele	Lānaʻi City	18	Resort	$225	☎808/565-4653

Golf

The spectacular oceanfront **golf courses** at Maui's major resorts, designed to tournament specifications but open to all, have the highest reputations, but they also have the highest green fees – all are well over $150, and the reductions for hotel guests are not all that significant. Rates at municipal courses, by contrast, can start as low as $40, while typical public courses charge upwards of $50 per round, with reduced rates early in the morning and later in the evening. All courses charge lower rates for Hawaii residents, and some charge extra premiums for foreign nationals. TeeTimes Hawaii (☎1-888/675-GOLF or 808/922-0431, ⊛www.teetimeshawaii.com) specializes in finding discounted and short-notice golfing opportunities.

You can find details of Maui's golf courses online at ⊛www.golf-maui.com, the website of the Maui Golf Shop (☎1-800/981-5512), which can also arrange discount rates.

Entertainment and festivals

Although island residents jokingly refer to the hour of 10pm as "Maui midnight," by Hawaiian standards Maui offers visitors a reasonably lively **nightlife**.

As ever, most of the activity is confined to the tourist enclaves, and the resort hotels in particular, but if you enjoy wandering the streets from bar to bar the oceanfront at **Lahaina** will be right up your street. The south coast, from **Kihei** on down, is too spread out to have the same intensity, but it's always party time somewhere along the strip – and especially around the downmarket but fun Kīhei Kalama Village mall.

Lovers of traditional Hawaiian music should head to the *Ritz-Carlton* in Kapalua, which stages an excellent series of weekly **slack key guitar** concerts, as described on p.71.

Away from the resorts, the local community of rock exiles and ex-Californians makes *Casanova's* in upcountry **Makawao** an amazingly happening venue for such a tiny town. There's also the Maui Arts and Cultural Center by the harbor in **Kahului**, which attracts big-name touring bands.

Festivals and events

Note that the exact dates of surfing contests, and in some cases the venues as well, depend on wave conditions.

January
Maui Pro Surf Meet; surfing competition, Honolua Bay and Ho'okipa Beach

3rd week in January
Hula Bowl Football All-Star Classic; college football tournament, War Memorial Stadium, Wailuku

Early February
Whale Fest Week; whale-related events, Lahaina and Kā'anapali

Late February
Maui Classical Music Festival, Maui Arts & Cultural Center

March
Run to the Sun; foot race, Pā'ia to Haleakalā

March/April
East Maui *Taro* Festival, Hāna

Late April
David Malo Day, Lahainaluna High School, Lahaina

Late April
Maui County Agricultural Trade Show, Ulupalakua Ranch

Late May
Bankoh Ho'omana'o Challenge; outrigger canoe race, Kā'anapali to Waikīkī International Festival of Canoes, Lahaina

Last Monday in May
In Celebration of Canoes, Lahaina

Mid-June
Maui Film Festival, Wailea

Late June
Kiho'alu; slack-key guitar festival, Maui Arts & Cultural Center

July 4
Makawao Rodeo, Makawao

Public holidays

Jan 1 New Year's Day
3rd Mon in Jan Martin Luther King Day
3rd Mon in Feb Presidents' Day
March 26 Prince Kuhio Day
Easter Monday
May 1 Lei Day
last Mon in May Memorial Day

June 11 Kamehameha Day
July 4 Independence Day
3rd Fri in Aug Admission Day
1st Mon in Sept Labor Day
2nd Mon in Oct Columbus Day
Nov 11 Veterans Day
4th Thurs in Nov Thanksgiving Day
Dec 25 Christmas Day

Early July
Quicksilver Cup; windsurfing competition, Kanahā Beach

Early August
Hawaii State Championships; windsurfing competition, Kanahā Beach

Mid-September
A Taste of Lahaina; food festival, Lahaina

Late September
Maui Marathon, Kahului to Kā'anapali

Early October
Maui County Fair, Wailuku

Mid-October
Aloha Festival

October 31
Halloween Mardi Gras of the Pacific, Lahaina

Late October/early November
Aloha Classic World Wavesailing Championships; windsurfing competition, Ho'okipa

Shopping

If you have come to Hawaii specifically to **shop**, the stores of Maui may not meet your needs. The state's premier malls are concentrated in Honolulu on Oahu, and unless you go there as well, you may fly home with fewer gifts and souvenirs than you expected. The prints, posters, and T-shirts on sale in Lahaina and the major tourist areas are OK if you think that whales are interplanetary voyagers from another dimension, or that a gecko on a surfboard is real neat, but stores and galleries selling high-quality indigenous arts and crafts are few and far between. Pā'ia and Makawao are the most likely towns to find interesting or unusual gifts.

Maui's largest malls are the Ka'ahumanu Mall and the Maui Marketplace in Kahului, though the most upmarket individual stores are in the Shops at Wailea mall, or in individual resort hotels.

Hawaiian Crafts

Some of the most attractive products of Hawaii are just too ephemeral to take home. That goes for the orchids and tropical flowers on sale everywhere, and unfortunately it's also true of *leis*.

Leis (pronounced *lays*) are flamboyant decorative garlands, usually consisting of flowers such as the fragrant *melia* (the plumeria or frangipani) or the Big Island's own bright-red *lehua* blossom (from the *'ō'hia* tree), but sometimes also made from feathers, shells, seeds or nuts. Both men and women wear them, above all on celebrations or gala occasions. The days are gone when every arriving tourist was festooned with a *lei*, but you'll probably be way-*leied* at a *lū'au* or some such occasion, while on Lei Day (May 1) everyone's at it.

Colorful Hawaiian clothing, such as the **aloha shirts** and the cover-all

"Mother-Hubbard"-style *mu'umu'u* dress, is on sale everywhere, though classic designs are surprisingly rare and you tend to see the same stylized prints over and over again. Sig Zane's store in Wailuku (see p.81) is the best source of out-of-the-ordinary *aloha* wear.

Otherwise, the main local crafts are **lau hala** weaving, in which mats, hats, baskets and the like are created by plaiting the large leaves (*lau*) of the spindly-legged pandanus (*hala*) tree, and **wood turning**, with fine bowls made from native dark woods such as *koa*.

Directory

Area code The telephone area code for the state of Hawaii is ☎808.

Electricity Hawaii's electricity supply, like that on the US mainland, uses 100 volts AC. Plugs are standard American two-pins.

Gay and lesbian life Much the greatest concentration of gay activism in Hawaii is in Honolulu, though the state as a whole is liberal on gay issues. Consensual "sodomy" is legal, with no criminal laws against private sex acts and a guarantee of privacy in the constitution. Maui hotels geared towards gay travelers include the *Sunseeker Resort* in Kīhei (see p.162). Pacific Ocean Holidays (PO Box 88245, Honolulu HI 96830-8245; ☎808/944-4700 or 1-800/735-6600, ⓦgayhawaiivacations.com) organizes all-inclusive **package vacations** in Hawaii for gay and lesbian travelers, and maintains the useful ⓦwww.gayhawaii .com website.

Hospitals Maui hospitals can be contacted on the following numbers: Wailuku ☎808/244-9056; Kula ☎808/878-1221; Hāna ☎808/248-8294. In emergencies call ☎911.

Inoculations No inoculations or vaccinations are required by law in order to enter

Hawaii, though some authorities suggest a polio vaccination.

Public toilets Some public toilets are labeled in Hawaiian: *Kanes* means Men, *Wahines* means Women.

Internet access Internet access is widely available. Most public libraries offer free access; hostels tend to have a computer or two where guests can check email; and both copier outlets and Internet cafés allow customers to go online.

Mail Mail service between Maui and the rest of the world is extremely slow, as all mail is routed via Honolulu. Allow a week for your letter to reach destinations in the US and as much as two weeks or more for the rest of the world. There are post offices in Lahaina at 132 Papalaua St, in the Lahaina Shopping Center (Mon–Fri 8.15am–4.15pm); in Kahului at 138 S Pu'uneēnē Ave (Mon–Fri 8.30am–5pm, Sat 9am–noon); in Wailuku at 250 Imi Kala St (Mon–Fri 8am–4.30pm, Sat 9am–noon); in Kīhei at the Azeka Shopping Center, 1254 S Kīhei Rd (Mon–Fri 8am–4.30pm, Sat 9am–1pm); and in Hāna at the Hāna Ranch Center (Mon–Fri 8am–4.30pm).

Quarantine Very stringent restrictions apply to the importation of all plants and animals into Hawaii. Cats and dogs must

Fly Less – Stay Longer!

Rough Guides believes in the good that travel does, but we are deeply aware of the impact of fuel emissions on climate change. We recommend taking fewer trips and staying for longer. If you can avoid travelling by air, please use an alternative, especially for journeys of under 1000km/600miles. And always offset your travel at ⓦwww.roughguides.com/climatechange.

International calls

To make an international call to Maui, dial your country's international access code, then 1 for the US, then 808 for Hawaii.

To place a call from Maui to the rest of the world, dial ☎011 then the relevant country code (Australia is 61;Britain 44; Canada 1; Ireland 353; New Zealand; 64).

stay in quarantine for 120 days; if you were hoping to bring an alligator or a hamster into the state, forget it. For full regulations contact the Hawaii Department of Agriculture (☎808/483-7151, ⓦwww.hawaii.gov/hdoa/ai/aqs/).

Senior travelers US residents aged 50 or over can join the American Association of Retired Persons (☎1-800/424-3410; ⓦ www.aarp.org), for discounts on accommodation and vehicle rental.

Telephones The telephone area code for the entire state of Hawaii is ☎808. Calls within Maui count as local; you don't need to dial the area code and it costs a flat-rate 50¢ on pay phones. To call another island, put ☎1-808 before the phone number; charges vary according to the time of day and distance involved.

Hotels impose huge surcharges, so it's best to use a phone card for long-distance calls. In preference to the ones issued by the major phone companies, you'll find it simpler and cheaper to choose from the various pre-paid cards sold in almost all supermarkets and general stores.

If you want to use your cellular or mobile phone on Maui, you'll need to check with your phone provider whether it will work there, and what the call charges are. Unless you have a tri-band phone, it is unlikely that a mobile bought for use outside the US will work inside the States, while some US phones only work within their local area code.

Smoking Smoking is banned in all restaurants and bars in Hawaii.

Time Unlike most of the United States, Hawaii does not observe Daylight Saving Time. Therefore, from 2am on the second Sunday in March until 2am on the first Sunday in November, the time difference between Hawaii and the US West Coast is three hours, not the usual two; the difference between Hawaii and the mountain region is four hours, not three; and the islands are six hours later than the East Coast, not five. Hawaiian time is from ten to eleven hours behind the UK. In fact it's behind just about everywhere else; although New Zealand and Australia might seem to be two and four hours respectively behind Maui time, they're on the other side of the International Date Line, so are actually almost a full day ahead.

Tipping Waiting staff in restaurants expect tips of fifteen percent, in bars a little less. Hotel porters and bellhops should receive at least $2 per piece of luggage and housekeeping staff at least $2 per night.

Travelers with disabilities The State of Hawaii Disability and Communication Access Board produces a wide range of reports on facilities for disabled travelers on each of the islands, which you can download from their website (☎808/586-8121, ⓦwww.state.hi.us /health/dcab/docs/TravelMaui.pdf). In addition, Access–Able (ⓦwww.access –able.com) carries detailed reports on the accessibility of hotels and other facilities throughout Hawaii.

Weddings To get married in Hawaii, you must have a valid state license, which costs $60 from the Department of Health, Marriage License Office, 1250 Punchbowl St, Honolulu HI 96813 (☎808/586-4545; ⓦwww.hawaii .gov/doh), and is valid for thirty days. You also need proof of rubella immunizations or screening, which can be arranged through the Department of Health. Most resorts offer their own marriage planners, while both the Maui Visitors Bureau (ⓦwww.visitmaui.com), and the Maui Wedding Association (ⓦwww .mauiweddingassociation.com) maintain full lists of Maui wedding service providers on their websites.

small print & Index

A Rough Guide to Rough Guides

In 1981, Mark Ellingham, a recent graduate in English from Bristol University, was traveling in Greece on a tiny budget and couldn't find the right guidebook. With a group of friends he wrote his own guide, combining a contemporary, journalistic style with a practical approach to travelers' needs. That first Rough Guide was a student scheme that became a publishing phenomenon. Today, Rough Guides include recommendations from shoestring to luxury and cover hundreds of destinations around the globe, including almost every country in the Americas and Europe, more than half of Africa and most of Asia and Australasia. Millions of readers relish Rough Guides' wit and inquisitiveness as much as their enthusiastic, critical approach and value-for-money ethos. The guides' ever-growing team of authors and photographers is spread all over the world.

In the early 1990s, Rough Guides branched out of travel, with the publication of Rough Guides to World Music, Classical Music and the Internet. All three have become benchmark titles in their fields, spearheading the publication of a range of more than 350 titles under the Rough Guide name, including phrasebooks, waterproof maps, music guides from Opera to Heavy Metal, reference works as diverse as Conspiracy Theories and Shakespeare, and popular culture books from iPods to Poker. Rough Guides also produce a series of more than 120 World Music CDs in partnership with World Music Network.

Visit www.roughguides.com to see our latest publications.

Rough Guide travel images are available for commercial licensing at www.roughguidespictures.com

Publishing information

This second edition published July 2008 by Rough Guides Ltd, 80 Strand, London WC2R 0RL. 345 Hudson St, 4th Floor, New York, NY 10014, USA.

Distributed by the Penguin Group
Penguin Books Ltd, 80 Strand, London WC2R 0RL
Penguin Group (USA), 375 Hudson Street, NY 10014, USA
14 Local Shopping Centre, Panchsheel Park, New Delhi 110017, India
Penguin Group (Australia), 250 Camberwell Road, Camberwell, Victoria 3124, Australia
Penguin Group (Canada), 10 Alcorn Avenue, Toronto, ON M4V 1E4, Canada
Penguin Group (NZ), 67 Apollo Drive, Mairangi Bay, Auckland 1310, New Zealand
Typeset in Bembo and Helvetica to an original design by Henry Iles.

Cover concept by Peter Dyer.

Printed and bound in China
© Greg Ward 2008

No part of this book may be reproduced in any form without permission from the publisher except for the quotation of brief passages in reviews.
192pp includes index

A catalogue record for this book is available from the British Library

ISBN 978-1-84353-989-6

1   3   5   7   9   8   6   4   2

Help us update

We've gone to a lot of effort to ensure that the second edition of Maui DIRECTIONS is accurate and up-to-date. However, things change – places get "discovered", opening hours are notoriously fickle, restaurants and rooms raise prices or lower standards. If you feel we've got it wrong or left something out, we'd like to know, and if you can remember the address, the price, the phone number, so much the better.

Please send your comments with the subject line "Maui DIRECTIONS Update" to ©mail @roughguides.com. We'll credit all contributions and send a copy of the next edition (or any other Rough Guide if you prefer) for the very best emails.
Have your questions answered and tell others about your trip at ©community.roughguides.com

Rough Guide credits

Text editor: Stephen Timblin
Layout: Umesh Aggarwal, Ajay Verma
Photography: Greg Ward
Cartography: Swati Handoo

Picture editor: Chrissy McIntyre
Proofreader: Anne Burgot
Production: Rebecca Short
Cover design: Chloë Roberts

The author

Greg Ward has written and taken photos for all five editions of the Rough Guide to Hawaii, and three previous Rough Guides to Maui, and also guides to the Big Island and Oahu, as well as Rough Guides to Las Vegas, Southwest USA, The Grand Canyon, Blues CDs, the History of the USA, and Brittany and Normandy. He has also co-written guides to the USA and Online Travel; edited the USA, India and Elvis guides among others; and worked for several other guide-book publishers.

Acknowledgements

Thanks so much to the many people who made researching this book such a pleasure, especially Candy Aluli, Nancy Daniels, and Michael Waddell. And heartfelt appreciation above all to Sam Cook, for all her support over the past year.

Thanks also to the great team at Rough Guides, and especially my ever-attentive editor Stephen Timblin; Annelise Sorensen; Katie Lloyd-Jones and the team in Delhi; and JJ Luck and Nicole Newman.

Index

Maps are marked in color

INDEX